T0259652

Spring Persistence
with Hibernate

Second Edition

Paul Fisher

Brian D. Murphy

Apress®

Spring Persistence with Hibernate, Second Edition

Paul Fisher
Brookyln, New York
USA

Brian D. Murphy
Maplewood, New Jersey
USA

ISBN-13 (pbk): 978-1-4842-0269-2

ISBN-13 (electronic): 978-1-4842-0268-5

DOI 10.1007/978-1-4842-0268-5

Library of Congress Control Number: 2016943012

Managing Director: Welmoed Spahr
Lead Editor: Steve Anglin
Technical Reviewer: Vinay Kumar
Editorial Board: Steve Anglin, Pramila Balan, Louise Corrigan, Jonathan Gennick, Robert Hutchinson,
    Celestin Suresh John, Michelle Lowman, James Markham, Susan McDermott, Matthew Moodie,
    Jeffrey Pepper, Douglas Pundick, Ben Renow-Clarke, Gwenan Spearing
Coordinating Editor: Mark Powers
Copy Editor: Kim Burton-Weisman
Compositor: SPi Global
Indexer: SPi Global
Artist: SPi Global

Distributed to the book trade worldwide by Springer Science+Business Media New York, 233 Spring Street, 6th Floor, New York, NY 10013. Phone 1-800-SPRINGER, fax (201) 348-4505, e-mail orders-ny@springer-sbm.com, or visit www.springeronline.com. Apress Media, LLC is a California LLC and the sole member (owner) is Springer Science + Business Media Finance Inc (SSBM Finance Inc). SSBM Finance Inc is a Delaware corporation.

For information on translations, please e-mail rights@apress.com, or visit www.apress.com.

Apress and friends of ED books may be purchased in bulk for academic, corporate, or promotional use. eBook versions and licenses are also available for most titles. For more information, reference our Special Bulk Sales–eBook Licensing web page at www.apress.com/bulk-sales.

Any source code or other supplementary materials referenced by the author in this text is available to readers at www.apress.com/9781484202692. For detailed information about how to locate your book's source code, go to www.apress.com/source-code/. Readers can also access source code at SpringerLink in the Supplementary Material section for each chapter.

Printed on acid-free paper

Contents at a Glance

Contents

About the Authors

Paul Tepper Fisher first began working in technology at Johns Hopkins University, where he spent several years developing a distance learning platform, while completing graduate school there. Currently, Paul is the CTO at *Recombine*, a genetics testing company in New York City with a mission to expand the scope and impact of genomics in medicine.

Before joining *Recombine*, Paul was the CTO at *Onswipe*, a mobile publishing platform, which was acquired by *Beanstock Media* in 2014. Prior to *Onswipe*, Paul was the CTO at *Sonar Media* — one of the first mobile social discovery platforms, which provided real-time notifications about relevant people nearby. Before joining *Sonar*, Paul was the CTO at *K2 MediaLabs*, a mobile-focused venture fund where he oversaw *K2*'s profile companies — including *Sonar*, *Marketsharing*, and *Tracks*.

Prior to *K2*, Paul was the Director of Engineering at *Lime Wire*, a Peer-to-Peer file-sharing company, where he led seven engineering teams for the development of a cloud-based Streaming Music Service. Previously, Paul managed the technology division for *Wired Digital* (owned by Condé Nast Publications), growing and overseeing the co-located development teams in both New York and San Francisco for *Wired.com*, *Webmonkey.com*, and *howto.wired.com*, helping *wired.com* triple its traffic to 12 million users.

In 2004, Paul founded *DialMercury.com*, a real-time communications and telephony platform. In 1998, Paul co-founded *SmartPants Media, Inc.*, a software development company focused on distance learning, video streaming, and interactive products, winning numerous awards, including a coveted *Muse Award* for the creation of an educational software application built for the Smithsonian Institution.

Paul has co-written two technology books, both published by Apress: *Spring Persistence — A Running Start*, and *Spring Persistence with Hibernate*.

Paul lives in Brooklyn, New York with his wife Melanie and daughter Madeleine.

Brian D. Murphy has been enamored with computers and programming since he got his first computer, an Apple IIc, in 1984. He graduated from Rutgers University with a BS in computer science. He has focused on web development in a variety of settings ranging from early-stage startups to large, multinational corporations in fields covering e-commerce, consulting, finance, and media. He was an early adopter of Spring and Hibernate, and he has used both frameworks on large production systems since 2003.

In his present role, Brian is the chief architect and director of engineering at Condé Nast, where he oversees the web and mobile presence for 25 award-winning brands, such as *WIRED*, *The New Yorker*, *Epicurious*, and *Vanity Fair*. He and his team leverage both Spring and Hibernate to power all of Condé Nast's online products, drawing tens of millions of unique visitors each month. Brian deals with the challenges of building and operating scalable, distributed systems every single day.

Brian lives in Maplewood, New Jersey, with his wife, Dania, son, Liam, and their dog, Cooper.

About the Technical Reviewer

Vinay Kumar is a technology evangelist. He has extensive, eight-plus years' experience in designing and implementing large-scale enterprise technology projects in various consulting and system integration companies. His passion helped him achieve certifications in Oracle ADF, WebCenter Portal, and Java/Java EE. Experience and in-depth knowledge has helped him evolve into a focused domain expert and a well-known technical blogger. He loves to spend time mentoring, writing technical blogs, publishing white papers, and maintaining a dedicated education channel on YouTube about ADF/WebCenter. In addition to experience in Java/Java EE, he is versed in various OpenStack technologies as well.

Vinay has contributed to the Java/Oracle ADF/WebCenter community by publishing more than 300 technical articles on his personal blog at www.techartifact.com. He was awarded Oracle ACE in June 2014. You can follow him at @vinaykuma201 or in.linkedin.com/in/vinaykumar2.

Acknowledgments

Writing a book always ends up being more difficult than you initially imagined. Although the absurdly late nights and lost weekends prove difficult to the authors, it is often the people around them that end up suffering the most. To that end, I'd like to thank Melanie Colton for her endless patience and perseverance. She deserves more than a medal for putting up with the many 4AM nights and my noisy typing. This book would not have been possible without her support and understanding. I also want to thank my amazing daughter, Madeleine — although she's too young to help copy-edit (or read) any chapters in this book, she inspires me every single day.

I would also like to acknowledge everyone I work with at Recombine for their continued trust and support. I consider myself lucky to have the opportunity to work with such a talented and dedicated team. I am grateful to be a part of such an important adventure.

I would be remiss if I didn't offer my appreciation and gratitude to my parents, who have inspired me through their relentless trust, support, and faith in everything I set out to do.

Finally, my sincere appreciation goes to Brian Murphy for joining the project and keeping things rolling along. If it hadn't been for Brian's tenacity and motivation, this book would never have seen the light of day. It's been an honor and privilege working with you again.

—Paul Tepper Fisher

We'd like to thank Apress for the opportunity to write this book. Special thanks to Steve Anglin for believing in us and letting us stretch the schedule to cover advanced topics in depth. We owe Mark Powers a special debt of gratitude for shepherding us through this process and ultimately dragging us across the finish line. Thanks to Matt Moodie, Marilyn Smith, and Sia Cyrus, who provided invaluable feedback, suggestions, and encouragement along the way. This is a much better book as a result of their wisdom and patience. Any issues or errors in this text are ours alone.

I would like to thank my wife, Dania, without whom this book wouldn't be possible. She graciously took on the role of super mom while I devoted nights and weekends to writing for far longer than bargained for. I'd like to thank my son Liam for being the most terrific little kid. You provide me with more joy and a new appreciation for the world than you'll ever know. I'd also like to acknowledge our second son, who is due shortly after this book will be published. I can't wait to meet you!

Lastly, I'd like to thank Paul Fisher for sharing this experience with me. This book was Paul's brainchild and I'm glad he invited me along for the ride. Writing this book has been both rewarding and challenging. I learned a ton and it's been great to work with you again.

—Brian D. Murphy

Preface

Since its inception, the Spring Framework has gradually changed the rules of application development in the Java community. This book is the ideal guide and teaching companion for developers interested in learning about the Spring Framework and how it can be leveraged to build persistence-driven applications using Hibernate, one of the most popular Java persistence frameworks today. *Spring Persistence with Hibernate* gets you rolling with fundamental Spring concepts, as well as proven design patterns for integrating persistence into your applications.

Many of the lessons illustrated in this book were culled from years of practical experience building scalable, high-volume web applications using Spring and Hibernate. One of the details that stands out in our joint experience is the importance and benefit of learning through hands-on experience. To this end, we will build a real-world application that utilizes Spring 4, Hibernate 5, Spring-Data, JPA 2.1, and Query-DSL. We firmly believe that learning about Spring and Hibernate implies far more than simply understanding the respective APIs of each framework. To be able to effectively develop with these two amazing technologies, it is necessary to understand the design patterns and best practices for getting the most from these frameworks, and building on them in a consistent, proven manner. We hope that this book teaches you more than just how to use Spring and Hibernate together. Our goal is to channel the development experience, lessons, and best practices we've seen work successfully in our experience, so that you can apply these skills and tools in your own applications.

Throughout these pages, we introduce core Hibernate fundamentals, demonstrating how the framework can be best utilized within a Spring context. We start with foundational concepts, such as strategies for developing an effective domain model and DAO layer, and then move into querying techniques using HQL, JPQL, Spring-Data, and Query-DSL (a powerful framework that offers a flexible, generic, and type-safe query abstraction). After fundamental concepts are introduced, we move on to more advanced topics, such as fetching and caching strategies. We also illustrate several approaches for architecting a transactional service facade. Both programmatic and declarative transactions are examined, showcasing the benefits of using Spring for expressing transactional semantics.

Spring Persistence with Hibernate also introduces JPA, covering its history and the ways in which Hibernate influenced its development. We discuss the benefits of following the JPA standard, as well as when it makes sense to utilize Hibernate-specific features. The book also examines different strategies and best-practices for architecting your persistence tier, such as illustrating the differences between the DAO and Active Record patterns. Throughout this book, we explore topics related to concurrency/optimistic locking, Hibernate Session state, caching approaches, and transaction management.

The last part of the book introduces several advanced techniques, important for working with enterprise Spring/Hibernate applications. We illustrate some of the pitfalls with integrating legacy databases, as well as best practices for developing REST web services, handling Hibernate proxies and lazy collections, and proven patterns that will prove valuable for any database-driven project running on the JVM.

Here are some of the main topics that we discuss in this book:

- Basic Spring Framework features such as IoC and AOP
- Core concepts for architecting a well-layered persistence tier
- JPA concepts and steps for integrating JPA
- Foundational and advanced concepts for working with Hibernate
- Hibernate querying techniques
- DAO and Service Facade layer development
- Building a REST web service
- Understanding the DTO pattern
- Leveraging other frameworks and technologies, such as Query-DSL
- Advanced caching and integration strategies

CHAPTER 1

Architecting Your Application with Spring, Hibernate, and Patterns

Persistence is typically the lifeblood of an application, providing the long-term memory that software requires in order to be useful across multiple invocations. Despite its importance, the architecture of a persistence tier is rarely granted adequate consideration during the design or implementation stages of an application. The consequences of this lack of planning can be far-reaching and devastating to an organization.

The primary goal of this book is to provide you with the best practices, tools, and strategies required to architect and implement a solid and effective persistence tier. Many of the concepts found on these pages were gleaned from real-world, practical experience designing and building web applications intended to scale to millions of daily users. Our objective is to illustrate the patterns and approaches that have worked for us, while examining the integration details for using Spring and Hibernate in your own applications.

One important lesson we've acquired over the years is that it's often best to learn by example. To this end, we will be building a real-world application over the course of the book: a Media Management web application, which allows users to create, edit, and view/listen to video, audio, and image files. To emphasize proven, pragmatic solutions and architectural patterns for building scalable and maintainable applications, each chapter will focus on a different aspect of application development, in regards to persistence. Through illustrated code samples and discussion, we will trace the design, architecture, and implementation of a real working application. Starting with the foundation, each successive chapter will build upon the previous one, adding new layers, features, and tests. And of course, as with any real-world application, we will do significant refactoring as we discover new capabilities of Spring and Hibernate, as well as alternative strategies and supporting frameworks.

The Benefit of a Consistent Approach

As you will learn throughout this book, the manner in which data is saved and queried is an integral part of every application. In fact, the persistence layer often serves as the foundation upon which an application is built. Building on top of this foundation are the three core components of a standard Spring-based persistence tier: the domain model, the Data Access Object layer, and the service layer. Don't worry if some of these terms are unfamiliar to you. In the upcoming chapters, we explain the purpose and function of each of these components, demonstrating the role each plays in an application.

While we don't suggest that there is only one correct approach to architecting an application, we do want to emphasize the benefit of using key design patterns and best practices. This is a theme that you will see cropping up over and over again.

Electronic supplementary material The online version of this chapter (doi:10.1007/978-1-4842-0268-5_1) contains supplementary material, which is available to authorized users.

P. Fisher and B.D. Murphy, *Spring Persistence with Hibernate*, DOI 10.1007/978-1-4842-0268-5_1

The Significance of Dependency Injection

The Spring Framework has helped to take much of the guesswork out of designing and building an application. It has become the de facto standard for integrating disparate components and frameworks, and has evolved far beyond its dependency injection roots. The purpose of dependency injection is to decouple the work of resolving external software components from your application business logic. Without dependency injection, the details of how a component accesses required services can get muddled in with the component's code. This not only increases the potential for errors, adds code bloat, and magnifies maintenance complexities; it couples components together more closely, making it difficult to modify dependencies when refactoring or testing.

By its very nature, Spring helps to enforce best coding practices and reduce dependency on external frameworks, or even classes within an application. At the simplest level, Spring is a lightweight IoC container, meaning that it will assume the responsibility of wiring your application dependencies. Exactly how this wiring responsibility is handled will be discussed in depth throughout this book. However, a theme you will see replayed throughout these pages is how Spring efficiently ties components together in a loosely coupled manner. This has far-reaching effects for any application, as it allows code to be more easily refactored and maintained. And in the context of this book, it allows developers to build a flexible persistence tier that is not directly tied to a particular implementation or framework.

Spring owes much of its success to the sheer number of integration points it provides, covering a wide range of frameworks and technologies. As developers realized the benefits gleaned from using Spring for integrating the various components within their own code, many new abstractions appeared that relied on Spring to integrate popular open source frameworks. Using Spring to integrate a particular framework not only simplifies the introduction of the framework, it allows the integration to be performed in a consistent manner — no different from the way collaborating components are wired within the context of an application. Additionally, using Spring's dependency injection to wire in a key framework ensures the integration is done in a decoupled way.

One of the leading catalysts for Spring's adoption was its support for the open source, object-relational mapping (ORM) framework, Hibernate. As the Spring Framework began to grow in popularity, the Java development community was also buzzing about Hibernate. It was a pivotal time for open source frameworks, as both Spring and Hibernate offered revolutionary solutions that would change the way many new applications were architected and implemented. As you will see, Spring and Hibernate complement each other in numerous ways, and each is partially responsible for the other's success and widespread adoption.

A Synergistic Partnership

In this book, we will focus on showing how Spring and Hibernate can be used together most effectively. Nevertheless, we will still emphasize strategies for decoupling Hibernate from your application. This is not because we have any concerns about using Hibernate, but rather because an architecture based upon a loose coupling of dependencies provides a cleaner separation of concerns.

No matter how good a framework might be, it's always better to keep dependencies decoupled. Not only does an agnostic persistence tier lead to better, cleaner, more maintainable code (as well as portability from one persistence technology to another), but it also ensures consistency across your application. Suddenly, your code is supported by a backbone that handles dependency wiring, provides aspect-oriented programming (AOP) capability, and generates cohesive configuration metadata that implicitly documents the way your application's pieces fit together.

Spring encourages design practices that help to keep all of your application's dependencies decoupled. Whether it be an external framework, an application component, or even Spring or Hibernate themselves, ensuring that collaborating components are not directly tied together helps prevent the concerns of one layer from leaking into another. By delegating all your wiring details to Spring, you not only simplify your code base by relieving the need to create infrastructural "access code," you also ensure that components are kept distinct. In the next few chapters, you will learn how coding to interfaces and using Spring's ORM abstractions and generic exception hierarchy can help to achieve these goals.

The Story of Spring's and Hibernate's Success

The rise in Spring's popularity stems from more than just its ability to reduce code complexity by helping to wire dependencies together. Much of the early excitement around the Spring Framework was due to its support for other leading open source frameworks, including Hibernate. Hibernate was one of the first open source ORM frameworks that provided an enterprise-level solution for building a persistence tier. Spring's ability to externalize integration details to an XML configuration file or express dependency injection through Java annotations provided a powerful abstraction that greatly simplified and standardized the integration efforts required to bootstrap Hibernate into an application.

ORM frameworks provide an abstraction layer over the actual persistence technology being used (usually a relational database), allowing developers to focus on the object-oriented details of their domain model, rather than lower-level database concerns. There is an inherent *impedance mismatch* between the relational-table world of databases and the object-oriented world of Java, making an effective ORM abstraction difficult to implement. This impedance mismatch is due to the fundamental differences between relational databases and object-oriented languages, such as Java. For example, relational databases don't implement core object-oriented principles such as polymorphism, encapsulation, and accessibility. Furthermore, the notion of equality is vastly different between Java and SQL. We will discuss some of these differences throughout this book, examining approaches to bridging the gap between a SQL database and a Java domain model.

Hibernate represented a significant step in bridging this gap by offering a powerful open source framework for expressing an object-oriented domain model, and defining the ways in which the tables and columns of a database synchronized with the object instances and properties in JavaBeans.

A Better Approach for Integration

Despite the improvements and efficiency with which a persistence tier could now be developed, integrating Hibernate into an application could still be a painstaking endeavor. With no standardized integration approach, developers were left to continuously reinvent the wheel, spending significant resources on the development and maintenance of the infrastructure code required to wedge Hibernate into their applications.

As Hibernate grew in popularity, the Spring Framework started to gain momentum as well. When Spring first came on the scene, its mission was to make the development of server-side Java applications simpler. First and foremost, it offered a better solution to wiring application dependencies together. For this reason, Spring is often referred to as a *container*, meaning that it offers a centralized abstraction for integrating collaborating dependencies via configuration, rather than writing (often repetitive) code to handle this task.

Part of Spring's momentum stems from the way it enables applications to deliver enterprise-level features, such as declarative transactions and security, without requiring the overhead and complexity of an Enterprise JavaBean (EJB) container or forcing developers to grapple with the details of specific technologies or standards. Time has proven EJB, although powerful in theory, to be a victim of overengineering. Spring and Hibernate owe much of their success to the fact that they provide a more reasonable and effective solution than the EJB standard. While Spring offers a simpler approach to declarative transaction management, Hibernate provides a more robust and intuitive ORM abstraction. Both frameworks were built and popularized by the growing need for a solution that was less complex than previous offerings. With the success of Spring and Hibernate came a stronger emphasis on building applications that were simpler and lighter weight, significantly increasing both ease of maintenance and scalability.

Although dependency injection was Spring's core purpose, the framework has evolved far beyond its original IoC foundation. The Spring Framework has expanded into other areas that naturally blend with its IoC roots. Spring now provides a pluggable transactional management layer, AOP support, integration points with persistence frameworks (such as Hibernate), a flexible web framework, called Spring MVC, and an ancillary framework aimed at standardizing and generifying data-access — across a range of different persistence technologies — called Spring Data. The addition of these features was a gradual process, spurred by demand and necessity.

As Hibernate's popularity surged, developers began to rely on Spring's persistence abstractions to simplify the often daunting task of integrating Hibernate into an application. Thanks to Spring, the process of getting up and running with Hibernate became a great deal easier. Developers could start with a Spring configuration file that not only bootstrapped a Hibernate `SessionFactory` (allowing configuration details to be specified via standard XML), but also streamlined the invocation of myriad Hibernate operations through the use of well-crafted abstractions founded on time-tested design patterns, such as `HibernateTemplate` and `OpenSessionInView`. We will discuss these core Spring/Hibernate integration details in the next few chapters. The important point here is that combining Spring and Hibernate affords developers an extremely powerful solution for persistence and data-access.

Not only does Spring simplify the integration of Hibernate, but it also reduces the coupling of Hibernate to an application. If the need arises to switch to a different ORM or persistence technology, this migration effort becomes much easier because there are few direct dependencies on Hibernate itself. For example, Spring provides a generic exception hierarchy for persistence-related errors. Although not required, it is considered good practice to convert Hibernate exceptions to Spring's generic exception hierarchy, which further decouples your application from Hibernate. Spring includes built-in mechanisms to simplify this conversion, to the point that it is fairly transparent. Additionally, Spring's integration code for other persistence technologies (such as JDBC, JPA, TopLink, etc.) will also handle the translation to Spring's generic exception hierarchy, further simplifying a migration from one persistence technology to another.

Establishing loosely coupled dependency relationships is one of Spring's core purposes. In fact, the framework itself limits direct coupling to itself as much as possible, meaning that your application will rarely be directly tied to Spring classes.

Best Practices for Architecting an Application

The more your code is abstracted away from interfacing directly with a database (and dealing with these lower-level concerns), the easier it is to switch to a different database or persistence technology. Similarly, Hibernate also offers an abstraction over your data model, allowing you to focus on your application's persistence details rather than on the particulars of your database. Through these decouplings, a persistence tier becomes far more portable across disparate databases.

Spring centralizes the wiring of dependencies within your application, making maintenance and configuration easier, and coercing developers to code to interfaces, which brings about cleaner and better code. It also allows you to focus more on your application's business logic, with less concern over how this information is physically stored and retrieved. This concept is often called *layering*. Each layer is focused specifically on accomplishing a particular task (with little knowledge or coupling to other layers within the application).

The Layers of a Persistence Tier

The application tier that deals with persistence is often called the *persistence tier*. Spring helps to enforce a modular architecture in which the persistence tier is divided into several core layers that contain the following:

- The domain model

- The Data Access Object (DAO) layer

- The service layer (or service facade)

Each of these layers is representative of proven design patterns that are key to building a solid, maintainable architecture. Outside the persistence tier, a typical Spring MVC application also has a controller layer, which handles user interaction (or powers a RESTful API), delegating to the service layer to handle the business logic, and then down to the DAO layer for lower-level persistence behavior. We will get into these implementation details over the next few chapters. Here, we'll take a brief look at the domain model, DAO, and service layers.

The Domain Model

The domain model represents the key entities within an application, defining the manner in which they relate to one another. Each entity defines a series of properties, which designates its characteristics, as well as its relationships to other entities. Each class within the domain model contains the various properties and associations that correlate to columns and relationships within the database. Typically, there is a domain entity for each table within the database, but this is not always the case.

For example, we might need to define a Person domain entity, designed to represent the concept of a *person* within the application and the database. The Person class could be represented as follows:

```
@Entity
public class Person implements Serializable {

    private Long id;
    private String firstName;
    private String lastName;
    private String username;
    private String password;
    private Integer roleLevel;

    private Integer version;

    public Person() {

    }

    @Id
    public final Long getId() {
        return id;
    }

    @Version
    public Integer getVersion() {
        return version;
    }

    . . . Remaining Getters and Setters Omitted
}
```

Part of Hibernate's job is to convert between domain model instances and rows in the database. Developers provide hints to help Hibernate perform these conversions, by specifying mapping rules using XML or annotations. This metadata is used by Hibernate to define the characteristics of the domain model and how the object-oriented properties within a domain model class map to columns and relationships within the database.

Although XML was initially used to define mapping rules, we recommend using annotations as this approach is simpler and more concise. In fact, by applying the @Entity annotation to a class, it is assumed that a class property should be persisted to the database using the property name as the database column name and using the field type as a hint for the database column type. Of course, this default behavior can be more explicitly configured or overridden entirely, but thanks to sensible defaults, your mapping configuration should be relatively terse most of the time.

While we strongly recommend leveraging annotations to define your domain model mappings, rather than the legacy XML-based approach, it is still useful to be familiar with both approaches since you may come across either strategy when working on older projects. Here is an example of the .hbm.xml (XML) mapping file for the Person entity defined earlier:

```
<hibernate-mapping>
    <class name="Person" table="person">
        <id name="id" type="long" column="id">
            <generator class="native"/>
        </id>
        <property name="firstName" column="first_name" type="string"/>
        <property name="lastName" column="last_name" type="string"/>
        <property name="username" column="user_name" type="string"/>
        <property name="password" column="password" type="string"/>
        <property name="roleLevel" column="role_level " type="integer"/>
        <version name="version" column="version" type="integer"/>
    </class>
</hibernate-mapping>
```

The Data Access Object (DAO) Layer

The DAO layer defines the means for saving and querying the domain model data. A DAO helps to abstract away those details specific to a particular database or persistence technology, providing an interface for persistence behavior from the perspective of the domain model, while encapsulating explicit features of the persistence technology. The goal of the DAO pattern is to completely abstract the underlying persistence technology and the manner in which it loads, saves, and manipulates the data represented by the domain model. The key benefit of the DAO pattern is separation of concerns—the lower-level details of the persistence technology and datasource are decoupled from the rest of the application, into a series of methods that provide querying and saving functionality. If the underlying persistence technology changes, most of the necessary changes would be limited to defining a new DAO implementation, following the same interface.

For example, we might create a PersonDao class to define all the application's persistence needs related to the Person entity. In PersonDao, we would likely have a method such as the following:

```
public Person findById(Long id);
```

This method would be responsible for loading a Person entity from the database using its unique identifier. The following might be another method for our application:

```
void save(Person person);
```

This method would be designed to handle all updates to a given row in the Person table (that is, creation or modifications).

When defining a DAO, it is good practice to first write the interface, which delineates all the core persistence-related methods the application will need. We recommend creating separate DAOs for each persistent entity in your domain model, but there are no clear rules in this area. However, defining DAO methods in a separate interface is crucial, as it decouples the purpose and contract of the DAO from the actual implementation, and even allows you to write more than one implementation for a given DAO interface.

It's important to note that such an interface is agnostic to the persistence technology being used behind the scenes. In other words, the interface only depends on the relevant domain model classes, decoupling our application from the persistence details. Of course, the DAO implementation class will use Hibernate, the Java Persistence API (JPA), or whatever persistence technology we have chosen to employ. However, the higher layers of our application are insulated from these details by the DAO interface, giving us portability, consistency, and a well-tiered architecture.

As we mentioned earlier, the Spring Framework also provides a generic data exception hierarchy, suitable for all types of persistence frameworks and usage. Within each persistence framework integration library, Spring does an excellent job of converting each framework-specific exception into an exception that is part of Spring's generic data-access exception hierarchy. All of the exceptions in Spring's generic exception hierarchy are unchecked, meaning your application code is not required to catch them. Spring helps to decouple your application from a particular persistence framework, allowing you to code to a generic and well-defined exception hierarchy that can be used with any persistence technology.

In Chapter 6, we will dive deeper into DAO implementation strategies, exploring the flexible querying and save/update capability afforded by Hibernate and JPA. Querying in particular can require quite a bit of complexity, and to this end, Hibernate and JPA provide alternative approaches for querying and accessing your data. HQL and JPQL (Hibernate Query Language and Java Persistence Query Language, respectively) both offer an object-oriented syntax for expressing queries that is very similar to SQL. Although concise and intuitive, HQL and JPQL are interpreted at runtime, which means you cannot use the compiler to verify the correctness and integrity of a query.

To address this limitation, Hibernate also includes a Criteria API, which allows queries to be expressed programmatically. Until recently, JPA did not offer a Criteria API, which meant developers would have to go outside the JPA standard if they required this type of querying facility. However, with the introduction of JPA 2.0, a Criteria API is now available as part of the standard.

As an additional option, Spring also provides support for QueryDSL, a flexible framework that offers a typesafe API for defining queries in a programmatic fashion. QueryDSL has the added benefit that its API provides a unified means for querying that works across a range of disparate persistence technologies, including JPA, JDO, Lucene, SQL, and MongoDB.

Whether to use HQL/JPQL, the Criteria API, or QueryDSL is sometimes a matter of style. However, there are some cases where a programmatic API (such as the Criteria API or QueryDSL) is more effective and maintainable. For instance, if you are building a feature that requires dynamic filtering or ordering, being able to create a query programmatically, based on the user's runtime specifications, is much cleaner than attempting to generate an ad hoc JPQL query string via concatenation. We will discuss these types of implementation decisions further in Chapter 6.

Leveraging Spring Data

Spring Data, one of Spring Framework's key subprojects, offers more flexible and efficient means for defining your application's DAO. By extending one of Spring Data's core interfaces, you can quickly incorporate useful querying and persistence capabilities for the relevant domain model. For instance, we could define our `PersonDao` interface through the following:

```
public interface PersonDao extends CrudRepository<Person, Long> {

}
```

This example provides our `PersonDao` with methods to persist and delete a `Person` entity, as well as basic querying capabilities (such as loading all `Person` entities, finding a `Person` instance by ID, etc.). Alternatively, we could also extend the `Repository` interface (from which `CrudRepository` also extends). This wouldn't provide us with the basic "CRUD" functionality that we were able to incorporate in the previous example. However, a powerful feature of Spring Data is the ability to define flexible queries simply by following a naming convention when defining our DAO methods. For instance, we could quickly create a method to query for all `Person` entities containing a first name of "Paul" by specifying a method:

```
public List<Person> findByFirstname(String firstname);
```

We can even incorporate powerful pagination capabilities by redefining the preceding method as follows:

```
public Page<Person> findByFirstname(String firstname, Pageable pageable);
```

Another alternative is to extend the `PagingAndSortingRepository`, which extends `CrudRepository` with `findAll` methods that provide flexible paging and sorting options.

We will learn more about these (and other) Spring Data features later in this book, but you should be able to infer that the `Page` and `Pageable` interfaces help to encapsulate the paging abstractions required to "chunk" a larger result set into smaller groups of "pages."

The Service Layer

The layer that handles the application business logic (surprisingly enough) is called the *service layer*. The service layer typically defines an application's public-facing API, combining one or more lower-level DAO operations into a single, cohesive transactional unit.

To help you understand how a service layer is built and used, let's take a look at a few examples:

```
Person loginUser(String username, String password);
```

The `loginUser()` method is intended to authenticate a user (that is, verify that the specified username and password match), and then load important user information into the session (grab user information, such as name, previous login date, role type, and so on). These tasks would likely not be handled by a single DAO method. Instead, we would probably build upon the functionality of two distinct DAO classes, a `PersonDAO` and a `RoleDAO`:

```
interface PersonDao {

    Person authenticateUser(String username, String password);

    . . .

}

interface RoleDao {

    Set<Role> getRolesForPerson(Person person);

    . . .

}
```

Together, these DAO methods accomplish a core business goal that is greater than the sum of its parts. In this example, we are using two read-only methods, but imagine a scenario in which we have a business method, such as the following:

```
boolean transferMoney(Long amount, Account fromAccount, Account destAccount)
  throws InvalidPermissionException, NotEnoughFundsException;
```

Now, assume that the preceding service layer method is composed of several DAO methods:

```
boolean validateSufficientFundsInAccount(Long accountId);
```

```
boolean removeFunds(Long accountId, Long amount);
```

```
boolean addFunds(Long accountId, Long amount);
```

It's easy to see what's going on here: we verify that enough cash exists in a particular account, and then pull the funds from one account and transfer them to another. The task is simple enough, but it doesn't take an overactive imagination to visualize the hysteria that might ensue should this business method fail halfway through the process—the funds might be withdrawn but never get deposited into the destination account. That might be good for the bank at first, but after a short while the entire economy collapses, and civilization is left with only a rudimentary barter system based on crazy straws and Star Wars action figures.

Leveraging Declarative Transactions

Service facade methods typically delegate to multiple DAO methods in order to accomplish some business logic as a single unit of work. This is the concept of a transaction: the entire method (and all of its side effects) completes 100 percent successfully, or the application is rolled back to the state before the method was called. Before Spring persistence came on the scene, transactional requirements often prompted developers to look toward EJBs, which let them declaratively configure transactional semantics for each facade method. When they cannot specify transactional requirements declaratively, developers must instead use a programmatic approach. Not only does this add code complexity and obscure the intentions of the persistence logic, it further couples the persistence technology to the application.

Transactional demarcation is often considered a *cross-cutting concern*, meaning it represents functionality that affects many parts of the codebase, but is orthogonal to their other features. Cross-cutting concerns add redundancy to code, since they need to be repetitively interwoven into the fabric of the business logic of an application, reducing code modularity. Aspect-oriented programming is aimed at solving this problem by allowing these concerns to be expressed once, and once only, as aspects, and then weaved into business logic as necessary.

In Spring, the service layer typically is intended to accomplish three primary tasks:

- Serve as the core API through which other layers of your application will interface (this is the incarnation of the facade pattern)

- Define the (typically coarse-grained) core business logic, usually calling on one or more finer-grained DAO methods to achieve this goal

- Define transactional details for each facade method

Understanding Aspect-Oriented Programming (AOP)

The service layer is where Spring's AOP support is best utilized. Spring ships with transactional support that can be applied to application code through the use of interceptors that enhance your service layer code, by weaving in the "transactional goodness." An interceptor is code that can be mixed into the execution flow of a method, usually delegating to the interceptor before and/or after a particular method is invoked. Simply speaking, an interceptor encapsulates the behavior of an aspect at a point in a method's execution.

It's not enough to specify that a method should be transactional. You shouldn't just force each method to occur within the confines of a transaction, rolling back if an error occurs and committing if all goes well. Perhaps certain methods don't attempt to modify any data, and therefore should execute within the context of a read-only transaction. Or more likely, perhaps some exceptions will trigger a rollback, while others will allow the transaction to carry on.

Pointcuts are another important component of Spring AOP. They help to define where a particular aspect (modularized functionality that can be weaved into application logic, such as transactional behavior) should be weaved. With Spring's transactional support, you have fine-grained control over which exceptions may trigger a commit or rollback, as well as the details over the transaction itself, such as determining the isolation level and whether a method should trigger a new transaction or a nested transaction, or execute within the existing transaction.

At a basic level, Spring accomplishes AOP through the use of the proxy design pattern. When you advise your classes by injecting cross-cutting behavior into various methods, you're not actually injecting code throughout your application (although in a way, that is the net effect of using AOP). Rather, you're requesting that Spring create a new proxy class, in which functionality is delegated to your existing class along with the transactional implementation (or whatever aspect you are trying to weave into your code). This explanation is an oversimplification of what actually happens under the hood, but the important thing to remember is that when you weave cross-cutting behavior into your classes via AOP, Spring is not directly inserting code; rather, it is replacing your classes with proxies that contain your existing code intertwined with the transactional code. Under the hood, this is implemented using Java Development Kit (JDK) dynamic proxies or CGLIB byte code enhancement.

Again, it's easy to see how this is a natural fit for a lightweight, IOC container like Spring. Since you're already entrusting Spring with handling your dependencies, it makes perfect sense to let Spring also take care of proxying these dependencies so you can layer on new cross-cutting behavior.

Although Spring AOP is amazingly powerful when you need to define and introduce new aspects to be weaved into your implementations, key transactional functionality is available out of the box and without the need to learn the details of AOP programming concepts. Still, understanding the basics of what Spring does under the hood is helpful. Keep in mind that AOP is useful for more than just applying transactional behavior—it is helpful for weaving any cross-cutting concern into your application, such as logging or security. We will discuss AOP in more detail later in this book.

Simplifying Transactions

Although applying transactions using Spring used to require a bit of AOP know-how, this process has been greatly simplified in recent versions of the framework. Now, applying transactional behavior to a service layer class is a matter of specifying the @Transactional annotation at either the class level or the method level. This annotation can be parameterized with attributes to customize its behavior; however, the most significant detail is whether a transaction is read-only (which means the transaction shouldn't attempt to perform inserts or updates).

Many developers don't recognize the importance of using transactions—even within a read-only context. Transactions can be useful for more than just ensuring atomicity of multiple database write operations. Transactions can also be used to specify a database isolation-level, and to delineate other contextual details that might be ambiguous outside a transactional scope. We strongly recommend that all database operations occur within the scope of some transaction—even if just to gain explicit control over the contextual state of the database. We will discuss some of these details, such as understanding isolation levels and advanced transactional options, when we examine transactions in more detail.

The Benefit of Coding to Interfaces

We can rely on Spring to wire DAO dependencies into our service layer classes, ensuring that this integration happens in a consistent way and that the integration point between these two layers is through interfaces rather than specific implementation classes. As we mentioned earlier in this chapter, this is a fundamental concept for leveraging Spring's dependency injection: by coding to interfaces, we get more for our money. We can always rely on Spring to automatically inject required dependencies, but by using interfaces, we gain the added benefit of being able to change which implementation should be injected at runtime. Without interfaces, there are no other options—we have hard-coded which dependencies must be injected into our components. Interfaces and Spring's dependency injection capability are a dynamic duo that offer significantly increased flexibility. For instance, without changing any code, you can choose to inject one set of dependencies for unit testing and another in production deployment. Or you can choose which implementations to use for each environment. These are some of the benefits afforded by adherence to best practices and leveraging the Spring Framework.

Testing Your Persistence Tier

As you'll see in later chapters, this separation of concerns helps keep your code clean and ensures that details from one layer don't interfere with the code from another layer. When it comes time for refactoring, this advantage can be significant. Perhaps even more important, these best practices are instrumental for ensuring an effective testing strategy. Over the course of this book, you will learn how Spring greatly simplifies the creation of unit and integration tests. When it comes to testing, it's rather intuitive to see how swapping implementations can really come in handy for mocking and stubbing. Spring 4 includes a powerful `TestContext` framework that simplifies the creation and management of unit and integration tests—even abstracting away which test framework you happen to be using.

Integration tests can often be a tricky matter, especially when you consider the details of instantiating all of a test's dependencies and components. For example, an integration test might require access to a database, as well as test data. Spring can bootstrap the `ApplicationContext` and then automatically inject any required dependencies. In the case of testing persistence-related code, you can choose to have your data occur within the scope of a transaction and then automatically rollback the transaction at the completion of the test to ensure that modifications made by the test are removed.

Advanced Features and Performance Tuning

This book will also cover some more advanced persistence concepts that are indispensable in most applications, such as optimization techniques for loading and managing complex relationships and collections within your domain model. We will discuss performance and optimization strategies, such as eager fetching and caching (at both the domain level and higher abstractions). As we mentioned earlier, Hibernate offers numerous features that can be leveraged to improve application performance. For instance, Hibernate and JPA offer a great deal of flexibility for tuning HQL/JPQL and Criteria API queries. These features enable developers to minimize round-trips to the database, allowing even large data sets to be accessed with minimal SQL queries. Hibernate also provides features such as lazy-loading, batching, and powerful caching mechanisms, which can be tuned to control the size and expiration time for cached entities. Understanding how these features work, as well as the myriad options available for controlling them, is critical for maximizing performance.

Caching is an often overlooked feature which can prevent an application from realizing its full potential. In the case of caching, it is either not fully utilized, or not enough time and attention are given to tuning and testing. However, if not configured properly, caching can actually significantly degrade application performance, or contribute to difficult-to-track-down bugs. In Chapter 9, you will learn how Hibernate caching works, strategies for tuning and improving performance, and how to integrate a cache provider, such as Ehcache. We will also explore several common pitfalls responsible for performance problems, such as the *N+1 Selects* issue, and how to go about identifying and resolving these issues.

Hibernate Search

Sometimes, your application will require more than what Hibernate or Spring have to offer. So we will discuss some important frameworks that extend Spring and Hibernate, such as Hibernate Search. Hibernate Search integrates Lucene, a popular open source search framework, into a Hibernate or JPA application. For features that require true search functionality, a relational database is not able to provide the capability that Lucene is able to offer. Hibernate Search seamlessly integrates Lucene into your persistence tier, allowing you to execute Lucene queries within the scope of a Hibernate Session or a JPA Persistence Context.

Hibernate Validator

Another relevant project that comes in handy for persistence-based applications is Hibernate Validator. Spring 4.1 offers the latest support for this useful framework, along with support for the Bean Validation Standard (for which Hibernate Validator is the reference implementation). Throughout the course of this book, we will be leveraging Hibernate Validator to define important constraints on our domain model in a declarative manner, which helps to streamline and simplify the application's business logic.

Building a REST Web Service

Since many applications use Spring and Hibernate as part of a web application, we will explore some of the potential issues and work-arounds related to building web applications. We will develop a REST-based web service, to explore some strategies for marshalling domain entities back and forth between Java and JSON or XML. In doing so, we will cover the latest support for JSON and XML marshalling in Spring 4, as well as Spring's powerful abstractions for building RESTful APIs (including its support for HATEOAS).

Other Persistence Design Patterns

Spring is based on time-tested design patterns, which go a long way toward simplifying code and reducing maintenance. While we're on the topic of some of the core building blocks of an application, let's look at a few of the more prevalent patterns used in much of the Spring architecture.

■ **Note**   You will see many of these patterns in action throughout this book, but it may be useful to take a look at the seminal work that popularized the use of patterns to solve recurring problems in object-oriented programming. This famous book is called *Design Patterns: Elements of Reusable Object-Oriented Software*, by Erich Gamma, Richard Helm, Ralph Johnson, and John Vlissides (Addison-Wesley, 1994). The authors, and by association their patterns, are often jokingly referred to as "The Gang of Four".

The Template Pattern

The Template pattern is one of the most frequently used idioms within Spring's ORM framework integration packages. Spring provides templates for each of the most popular persistence frameworks, making it easy to port your code to a different persistence implementation. The Template Pattern is also used by the Spring framework to more effectively integrate JMS, define transactional behavior, and provide outbound email message capability, among other things.

The Template pattern allows a template to be defined in which a series of standard steps are followed, delegating to a subclass for those operations that are specific to the business logic. For example, when working with Hibernate, it is first necessary to create and initialize a new Hibernate session and optionally begin a transaction, before executing any Hibernate operations. When the operations are completed, it is necessary to close the session, and optionally commit or rollback the transaction. It would be rather redundant to repeat these same steps each time it was necessary to interface with Hibernate. Instead, we can leverage Spring's HibernateTemplate or JpaTemplate abstractions, which handle these steps for us. Although using these template support classes is an effective approach, we will explore alternative options later in this book.

Typically, a template is defined as an abstract class. To specify the operations to be wrapped within the templated workflow, we extend the template class, providing or extending the implementations for the abstract methods defined in the template parent class.

The Template pattern does exactly what its name implies: it extracts boilerplate and redundant tasks into a template, delegating to your specific implementation for functionality that can't be templated. In most cases, the code that cannot go in a template is your persistence logic itself. Using the Template pattern means you can focus on the database operations, without needing to worry about some of these mundane details:

- Opening a database connection

- Beginning a transaction

- Wrapping your SQL operations in try-catch blocks (to handle unexpected exceptions)

- Committing or rolling back a transaction

- Closing the database connection (and handling any exceptions during this process)

- Catching any exceptions that might occur in the transaction

Without using Spring, much of your code has little to do with your persistence logic, but is the same boilerplate code required by each and every operation.

Spring's HibernateTemplate and JpaTemplate offer a series of convenience methods to streamline much of the common persistence-related functionality. For example, the HibernateTemplate provides some useful methods such as:

- *saveOrUpdate(Object entity)*

- *load(class entityClass, Serializable id)*

- *find(String hqlQuery)*

- *findByCriteria(DetachedCritieria criteria)*

- *delete(Object entity)*

HibernateTemplate offers quite a few more methods, as well as numerous permutations of some of the methods listed earlier. However, these convenience methods aren't direct examples of the template pattern. Rather, they are more like wrapper methods, which delegate to the core template method found in Spring's HibernateTemplate abstraction:

```
    @Override
public <T> T execute(HibernateCallback<T> action) throws DataAccessException {
    return doExecute(action, false);
}
```

To execute a series of Hibernate operations, ensuring that they occur within the necessary templated steps (such as initializing and closing a Hibernate session), we need to create an anonymous implementation of the HibernateCallback interface, which is the single parameter to the preceding execute method. For example, to save an entity to the database, we could do the following:

```
public void customSavePerson(Person person) {
  getHibernateTemplate().execute(
    new HibernateCallback<Person>() {
      public Person doInHibernate(Session session) throws HibernateException {
        session.saveOrUpdate(person);
      }
    }
  );
}
```

Of course, it would be a lot simpler to just use HibernateTemplate's save(Object entity) method. Yet in this contrived example, we define an implementation of the HibernateCallback interface, which uses the passed-in Session to persist the Person entity to the database. Typically, this type of lower-level persistence functionality would be part of a DAO class, which helps to abstract the Hibernate-specific code from the rest of the application.

Although the HibernateTemplate and JpaTemplate provide an effective construct for streamlining persistence operations, they are no longer as necessary as they once were. Hibernate 3 shipped with a feature called Contextual Sessions, which provides greater flexibility around the scope of a Session. Part of what Spring's ORM support provides is the facilitation of a conversation surrounding persistence behavior, allowing Hibernate and JPA operations to be seamlessly integrated into Spring's transactional support. Spring's transactional features couldn't be properly utilized if every Hibernate operation created a new Session and a new database connection. To tie multiple lower-level persistence operations into a holistic "conversation," Spring uses the capabilities of ThreadLocal, allowing disparate operations to be scoped across a continuous thread. Recent versions of Hibernate provide a pluggable mechanism for defining how accessing the current Session should work. This new capability makes the HibernateTemplate and JpaTemplate a bit redundant in some circumstances. We will discuss the benefits and drawbacks of Spring's ORM templates in the next few chapters.

■ **Note** Spring can be used for both JTA-managed transactions and local resource transactions. In a JTA environment, transactions are managed by the container, and offer additional behavior, such as distributed transactions. However, there is additional overhead for leveraging JTA transactions, and we recommend going with lighter-weight, local transactions if your application doesn't require the features provided by JTA. One of the advantages of using Spring is that switching between locally managed transactions and JTA is just a matter of configuration. In the case of JTA, Spring will simply delegate to JTA, rather than manage the contextual state across an application thread.

The Active-Record Pattern

The DAO pattern isn't the only strategy for performing data operations. Another approach that has started to garner more attention recently is the Active-Record pattern. Active-Record is a design pattern popularized by frameworks such as Ruby on Rails and Grails, and takes a different approach than abstracting persistence functionality into a separate layer. Instead, Active-Record attempts to blend a domain object's behavior directly into the domain class itself.

Typically, an instance of a particular domain class represents a single row within the respective database table. To save changes to the instance (and thereby the appropriate row within the database), a save instance method is called directly on the instance. To delete an instance, we can simply invoke delete() on the instance that needs to be deleted. Query operations are usually invoked as static methods on the domain class itself. For example, in Grails, to find all Person entities with a lastName property of Fisher, we could call Person.findAllByLastName('Fisher').

The benefit of Active-Record is that it provides an object-oriented, intuitive, and concise approach for performing persistence operations, and usually reduces code overhead significantly. Although the Active-Record pattern is fundamentally different from the DAO pattern, you probably recognize some similarities in how the Spring Data method-naming conventions allowed for an effective and intuitive means for defining queries. We will continue to explore and contrast these (and other) strategies for defining queries and persistence behavior throughout this book.

Summary

Throughout this book, we will demonstrate how Spring integrates with key persistence frameworks and strategies. Along the way, you will learn more about Spring's features and capabilities, and some of the key design patterns it uses to get the job done effectively.

Until several years ago, simple Java Database Connectivity (JDBC) was one of the most popular choices for implementing an application's persistence tier. However, EJB and open source ORM frameworks such as Hibernate have significantly changed the persistence landscape, by allowing developers to focus on a Java-based domain model, maintaining the object-oriented semantics of Java while still working with the relational concepts of a SQL database. ORM offers a level of abstraction that affords increased flexibility by decoupling application code from the lower-level details of a relational database.

However, things aren't always as easy as they seem. ORM is not without its drawbacks and consequences. First, as we mentioned earlier, there is the impedance mismatch between the object-oriented Java world and the relational SQL world. ORM frameworks, such as Hibernate, do their best to address this mismatch by offering extensive options for mapping between SQL and Java. Nevertheless, fundamental differences between these two spheres will always exist, and therefore can't be fully addressed.

Despite some of these limitations, ORM frameworks offer unparalleled benefits by streamlining the way in which developers work with a relational database. For instance, Hibernate introduces ancillary features, such as caching and lazy loading, which can improve the performance of an application dramatically with little or no additional coding effort. Hibernate and JPA also provide tools to seamlessly generate database schemas and even keep them in sync with the Java-based domain model. These features make the integration between application code and database even more seamless—to the point that it is often possible to forget that you are using a database altogether!

With an IoC container at its core, Spring helps to reduce application complexity, as well as coupling between classes, by handling the details necessary to integrate one dependency with another. Spring also provides transactional behavior, AOP capability, and infrastructural classes for numerous persistence frameworks, such as Hibernate and JPA.

Hibernate is an ORM framework intended to translate between relational databases and the realm of object-oriented development. Hibernate provides a querying interface, using Hibernate Query Language (HQL) or the Hibernate Criteria API. Together, Spring and Hibernate are a dynamic duo, capable of simplifying dependency collaboration, reducing coupling, and providing abstractions over persistence operations.

JPA is a Java standard for persistence, the design of which was significantly influenced by the Hibernate developers. Hibernate can be used as an implementation provider for JPA, allowing you to adhere to standards and gain framework portability, while still utilizing the excellent Hibernate implementation. However, there are some useful features that are not available in JPA, but are present only in the Hibernate implementation. With the release of JPA 2.0, many of the limitations of the JPA spec have been addressed, bringing more parity to Hibernate and JPA. For instance, JPA 2.0 now provides a Criteria API for querying in an object-oriented manner, and compile-time checking.

In this chapter, we outlined the foundational layers of a typical persistence tier, which is composed of the domain model, the DAO layer, and the service facade. We also discussed some integral design patterns leveraged by the Spring Framework, such as the Template design pattern. Although adhering to the typical foundational layers for your persistence tier is usually the best approach, some newer frameworks follow slightly different strategies, such as using the Active-Record pattern.

In the next chapter, we will build on the concepts and patterns introduced in this chapter as we incrementally build a Gallery application using Spring and Hibernate. Over the course of this book, it is our aim to illustrate time-tested and pragmatic best practices that we hope you will be able to use in your own applications as well.

Before we start coding, it's important to understand some of the core Spring and Hibernate concepts. So in the next chapter you will learn about Spring's architecture and capabilities, such as dependency injection, AOP, and persistence-related features.

CHAPTER 2

Spring Basics

The Spring Framework has its origins in the companion code for Rod Johnson's book, *Expert One-on-One J2EE Design and Development* (Wrox, 2002). The book developed a strong following of developers, who used the Wrox forums to discuss both the book and the corresponding code. Two of those developers, Juergen Hoeller and Yann Caroff, persuaded Rod to turn the code into an open source project. The book referred to the framework as the Interface21 framework, because Rod felt that it represented the future of enterprise Java development—a framework for the twenty-first century. However, when the open source project was formed, they felt they needed a name that could better inspire a community. Yann suggested Spring because of the association with nature, as well as the fact that Spring represented a fresh start after the "winter" of traditional J2EE development. The project went public in 2003, and version 1.0 of the Spring Framework was released in 2004.

Since then, Spring has been widely adopted because it delivers on the promise of simpler development while also tackling some very intricate problems. Another key to Spring's rise to prominence is its exceptional documentation. Many open source projects have faded into oblivion because of the lack of sound documentation. Spring's documentation has been very mature since the very early days of the project.

Despite what some may claim, the Spring Framework is not currently a standard. Standard technologies are great, and Sun Microsystems (and now Oracle, which acquired Sun in 2010) deserves a lot of credit for pushing standards-based Java technologies into the mainstream. Standards allow you to do things like develop your web application on Tomcat (an open source web container — or application server) implementation that conforms to the Servlet Container Standard) and then drop it into WebSphere (a proprietary Java EE container, maintained by IBM), with little adjustment required (at least theoretically). But even though the Spring Framework is unbelievably popular today, it does not represent a true standard.

Some consider Spring a *de facto standard*, due to the sheer volume of applications that rely on it. Spring provides a means for integrating the various components of your application in a consistent way, and it is deployed far and wide across a variety of application ecosystems. Sometimes, this type of *standard implementation* is a far more valuable proposition than a *standard specification*.

Despite the naysayers that balk at the idea of using any technology that wasn't designed by a giant committee of corporate volunteers, using Spring in your application poses little risk. In fact, the more you utilize Spring for integrating components into your application, the more consistent your integration strategy will be, making maintenance and development easier. That's right—reliance on Spring will often lead to better, cleaner, decoupled code. In fact, an application that adheres to most of the Spring Framework's best practices should have little coupling to the framework, as one of Spring's primary purposes is to encourage modularization and decoupling of code dependencies — including minimizing dependencies on Spring itself. Throughout this book, you learn how to adopt and leverage these best practices throughout all facets of an application (including tests as well).

Because Spring is such a large framework, and because the documentation is so good, we have no intention of covering it all. Instead, this chapter will serve as a quick overview of the most important concepts that we build on in the rest of this book.

P. Fisher and B.D. Murphy, *Spring Persistence with Hibernate*, DOI 10.1007/978-1-4842-0268-5_2

Exploring Spring's Architecture

Spring is composed of a series of modules. The beauty of this design is that you can pick and choose the components that you would like to use. There's no monolithic JAR file. Instead, you explicitly add the components that you want to your project dependencies.

As they say, a picture is worth a thousand words. Figure 2-1 is a depiction of the Spring components. The three primary groupings are the core, web, and data access modules.

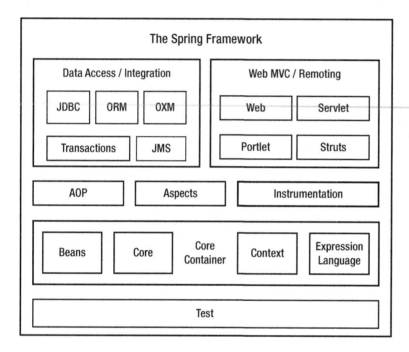

Figure 2-1. *The Spring Framework modules*

We'll be tackling many of these modules in this book. This chapter will take you through the core container and AOP.

The Application Context

Spring's job is to parse your configuration files and then instantiate your managed classes, resolving their interdependencies. Spring is often called a *container*, since it is designed to create and manage all the dependencies within your application, serving as a foundation and context through which beans (which represent the dependencies, or collaborators, within your application) may be resolved and injected where necessary—or even explicitly looked up, when necessary. This core engine is represented by a base interface called BeanFactory.

The BeanFactory interface defines the core Spring engine that conglomerates your beans and wires the collaborating dependencies together. But the Spring container is capable of much more than just dependency injection. It can also be used to publish events, provide AOP functionality, support a resource-loading abstraction, facilitate internationalization, and so on. For many of these advanced capabilities, you will need to use an ApplicationContext instance.

The `ApplicationContext` extends the `BeanFactory` interface, providing a set of more robust features. The separation can come in handy if you are building a very lightweight application and you don't need some of these more advanced features. But for most applications (especially server-side software), you will want to use an `ApplicationContext` implementation. In the case of web applications, you will typically use a `WebApplicationContext`.

Prior to the Servlet 3.0 standard, it was necessary to configure your web application's `web.xml` file to properly bootstrap a Spring `WebApplicationContext`. Since Servlet 3.0 (and Spring 3.1), it is also possible to bootstrap a `WebApplicationContext` programmatically through the use of a `WebApplicationInitializer`. Although it is becoming increasingly more popular to take the more programmatic approach (which eschews the need to configure a `web.xml` altogether—or even a Spring XML-based configuration), we will examine both approaches, since there are merits and drawbacks for each.

An XML-Based Approach

Spring ships with a listener that you can throw into your `web.xml` file to automatically bootstrap the Spring `ApplicationContext` and load your Spring configuration. It's as easy as adding the following lines into your `web.xml`:

```
<listener>
    <listener-class>
        org.springframework.web.context.request.RequestContextListener
    </listener-class>
</listener>
```

These lines will ensure that Spring is loaded when your application first starts up and will parse the configuration file located at `WEB-INF/applicationcontext.xml`.

If you're not building a web application, it's just as easy to load the Spring container. In this case, we recommend going with the `ClassPathXmlApplicationContext` implementation, which is designed to load the Spring configuration files from the classpath. It is invoked in the following way:

```
ApplicationContext context =
    new ClassPathXmlApplicationContext(new String[]{"configfile1.xml", "configfile2.xml"});
```

You can see just how easy it is to get a Spring container instantiated. Once you have a reference to the `ApplicationContext`, you can use it however you wish. The reference that is returned to you is the loaded `ApplicationContext`, with all the beans that you defined instantiated and dependencies resolved.

If you felt so inclined, you could access a bean by name, simply by invoking the following:

```
UsefulClass usefulClass =  (UsefulClass) context.getBean("myBeanName");
```

Assuming that your bean is defined somewhere in your Spring configuration files (referenced by the ID or name attribute), Spring will hand you your class instance, ready to go (meaning all of its dependencies will have been injected). However, we strongly recommend that you try to avoid issuing calls to `getBean()`.

The whole point of Spring is automatic dependency injection, which means not looking up your beans when you need them. That's dependency lookup, which is so 1995. While this approach does decouple and defer your class dependencies, it still requires an explicit lookup step. As a rule of thumb, if you need a reference to a particular dependency, specify these details in the configuration, not in your code.

Some developers rely on `getBean()` only in circumstances in which they *always* need a new instance of their class (each time they make the call). A better solution to this problem is using the `lookup-method` property in your XML configuration. This property coerces Spring to override or implement the specified method with code that always returns a new instance of a designated bean.

An alternate strategy for accessing beans from the ApplicationContext is to implement the ApplicationContextAware interface. This interface has the following method:

```
void setApplicationContext(ApplicationContext context);
```

With access to Spring's ApplicationContext, your class has the flexibility to look up beans by name or type, without you needing to write code to acquire an ApplicationContext from the classpath directly. In practice, there shouldn't be many cases where you need to integrate Spring's API so deeply into your code. The more common approach is to let Spring manage the relationships between beans dynamically through dependency injection.

Code-Based Configuration

While an XML-based configuration was the original approach when the Spring Framework first came on the scene, a Java-based configuration method is becoming increasingly popular. That said, there are still pros and cons for each strategy. For instance, an XML-based approach is often terser and has the added benefit of living outside your application's code base. This allows an XML configuration to change without requiring recompilation of the code base.

Java-based configuration, however, provides you with the full flexibility and compile-time safety of Java, along with key features not afforded by XML. We will explore Java-based configuration later in this chapter.

Beans, Beans, the Magical Fruit

A big part of the secret sauce for the Spring Framework is the use of Plain Old Java Objects, or POJOs. Martin Fowler, Rebecca Persons, and Josh MacKenzie originally coined the term POJO in 2000. POJOs are objects that have no contracts imposed on them; that is, they don't implement interfaces or extend specified classes.

There is often quite a bit of confusion about the differences between JavaBeans and POJOs. The terms tend to be used interchangeably, but that's not always accurate. JavaBeans are best characterized as a special kind of POJO. Put simply, a JavaBean is a POJO that follows three simple conventions:

- It is serializable.

- It has a public, a default, and a no argument constructor.

- It contains public getters and setters for each property that is to be read or written, respectively (write permissions can be obscured simply by defining a getter, without defining a setter).

An object in Java may be a POJO but not a JavaBean. For instance, it may implement an interface or extend specified classes, but because it refers to objects that are stateful and/or exist outside the scope of the Java Virtual Machine (JVM)—for example, HTTP or database connections—it cannot reasonably be serialized to disk and then restored.

The concept of JavaBeans was originally devised for Swing to facilitate the development of stand-alone GUI components, but the pattern has been repurposed for the land of Spring beans and back-end persistence with Hibernate.

The Spring Life Cycle

Spring not only instantiates objects and wires up dependencies, but it also handles each managed object's *life cycle.*

For example, what if you need to do some initialization in your class after the Spring-injected properties have been set? One way to accomplish this is through constructor injection (so that you can capture the moment all of a bean's properties are injected). However, an alternative approach is to use the init-method feature. By defining an init-method attribute on your bean, you can specify an arbitrary method that will be called after all of the Spring properties have been set (that is, after all of your setters have been invoked). Here is an example of using the init-method feature of Spring:

```
<bean id="initTest" class="com.apress.springpersistence.audiomanager.InitTest"
init-method="init">
    <property name="testString"  value="Let me out of this computer!"/>
</bean>
```

Simple, right? Next, we need to define a class with the init-method that specified in the preceding configuration:

```
package com.apress.springpersistence.audiomanager;

import org.springframework.util.Assert;

class InitTest {

    private String testString;

    public void init() {
        // let's do some initialization stuff!
        Assert.notNull(this.testString,
                    "You forgot to set the testString property! What were you
                    thinking???");
    }

    public void doBizLogic() {
        ...
    }

    public void setTestString(String testString) {
        this.testString = testString;
    }

    public String getTestString() {
        return this.testString;
    }

}
```

If you're using Java 5 or later, you can also tap into Spring's annotation support for initialization events. Using this approach, you simply annotate a class's methods with the @postConstruct annotation, without needing to specify initialization hints in the Spring configuration. For example, you could refactor the earlier example as follows:

```
package com.apress.springpersistence.audiomanager;

import org.springframework.util.Assert;

class InitTest {

    private String testString;

    @PostConstruct()
    public void init() {
        // let's do some initialization stuff!
        Assert.notNull(this.testString,
                    "You forgot to set the testString property! What were you
                    thinking???");
    }

}
```

As with everything in Spring, there's actually more than one way to skin a cat. Instead of specifying init-method in the configuration or using the @postConstruct annotation, you could have your class implement the InitializingBean interface. To a certain extent, using this interface makes things a bit easier, since you don't even need to change your configuration. The interface just requires you to implement an afterPropertiesSet() method, which is automatically detected and called for you once Spring has finished setting all the configured properties. The downside with this approach is that you sacrifice your simple POJOs and tightly couple your beans to Spring. While coupling to Spring isn't terrible, the cleaner approach is to keep initialization details entirely within configuration and out of the code. So let this be your mantra: *keep it in the configuration.*

Similar to acting on bean creation, you may also trigger custom logic when beans are destroyed. You can accomplish this in several ways:

- By implementing the DisposableBean interface, which is essentially the inverse of InitializingBean

- By applying a @preDestroy annotation to the method in question

- By configuring the destroy-method parameter in your Spring XML configuration, which is what we recommend to minimize tight coupling

Now that you know how to tap into the creation and destruction life-cycle events in Spring, there's another aspect of bean management that's crucial to understand when building enterprise applications: bean scoping.

Understanding Bean Scopes

By default, beans defined in Spring are all scoped as singletons. A *singleton* is a class that is guaranteed to have only a single instance in the JVM. Singletons are great for storing application state, or for any situation where you want to be assured that there is only ever one reference in your application. Normally, you would need to write code to achieve this assurance.

The typical singleton meets the following criteria:

- It has a static method to return the single instance of the class (stored as a static reference within the class)

- It has a private constructor, ensuring that only the singleton itself can ever create a new instance (which is your assurance that you won't accidentally create more than once instance simply by invoking new Singleton())

A singleton in your application might look like this:

```
public class Singleton {
    private static final Singleton INSTANCE = new Singleton();
    private Singleton() {
    }
    public static Singleton getInstance() {
        return INSTANCE;
    }
}
```

Although the preceding sample illustrates a useful design pattern, Spring obviates the need to write this boilerplate code, once again allowing you to move these details into the configuration. By default, all Spring beans are singletons. If this is not your intention, you need to specify a different scope for your bean.

In Spring 1.*x*, beans were either prototype beans or singletons. *Prototype* means that each new call to getBean() will return a brand-new instance of your bean. Singleton beans guarantee that there can only ever be a single instance of your class in the entire Spring ApplicationContext. Spring 2.*x* introduced several new standard scopes, as well as the ability to define custom scopes. Spring 3.*x* added a thread scope, though it's not registered by default. Table 2-1 lists the bean scopes that are provided by Spring out of the box.

Table 2-1. *Spring Bean Scopes*

Scope	Description
Singleton	Scopes a single bean definition to a single object instance per Spring IoC container. This is the default scope.
Prototype	Scopes a single bean definition to any number of object instances.
Request	Scopes a single bean definition to the life cycle of a single HTTP request; that is, each HTTP request has its own instance of a bean created off the back of a single bean definition. This scope is valid only in the context of a web-aware Spring ApplicationContext.
Session	Scopes a single bean definition to the life cycle of an HTTP session. This scope is valid only in the context of a web-aware Spring ApplicationContext.
Global session	Scopes a single bean definition to the life cycle of a global HTTP session. This scope is valid only in the context of a web-aware Spring ApplicationContext, and typically only in a portlet context.
Simple thread	If for some reason, the request, session, or global session scopes don't satisfy your needs, you may enable the simple thread scope to bind a bean definition to an instance of ThreadLocal.

So now you know how to create beans in the Spring ApplicationContext and manage their scope and life cycle. The next piece of the puzzle is how to retrieve those beans from the Spring container within your application.

Dependency Injection and Inversion of Control

Enterprise applications are composed of many objects that provide behavior to emulate business processes. Two very important design patterns have emerged to manage the relationships between objects in an object-oriented application:

- *Dependency injection (DI)*: Classes that employ dependency injection specify the objects that they interact with through constructor arguments, factory method parameters, or public mutators (aka *setters*). With a dependency-injection container or framework like Spring, the ability to externalize simple class properties is just the beginning. Developers can create a complex tree of dependencies, leaving the work of figuring out how each dependency is created and set (also called *injected* or *wired*) to the Spring lightweight container.

- *Inversion of Control (IoC)*: When object location or instantiation is removed as a responsibility for a given bean and instead left to the framework, control has been *inverted*. This inversion of control is a very powerful concept and represents the foundation on which the Spring Framework is based.

Dependency injection and IoC lead you down a path toward clean code that embodies high cohesion and loose coupling.

Setter-Based Dependency Injection

Although frighteningly simple, Spring's use of POJOs as a means of configuration and integration is quite powerful. Consider the example of a fictitious User bean, which could be used in an application to specify user credential information:

```xml
<?xml version="1.0" encoding="UTF-8"?>
<beans xmlns=http://www.springframework.org/schema/beans
       xmlns:xsi=http://www.w3.org/2001/XMLSchema-instance
       xsi:schemaLocation="http://www.springframework.org/schema/beans
           http://www.springframework.org/schema/beans/spring-beans-4.1.xsd">

    <bean id="userBean" class="com.apress.springpersistence.audiomanager.core.domain.User">
        <property name="username" value="admin" />
        <property name="password" value="password" />
    </bean>

</beans>
```

You can take away several things from the preceding example. The first is that we use horribly insecure passwords. Nevertheless, it does demonstrate how a simple Spring bean is configured via XML.

To make this work on the Java side, you need a valid JavaBean class that looks like the following:

```
package com.apress.springpersistence.audiomanager.core.domain;

public class User implements Serializable {

    private String username;
    private String password;

    public User() {
    }

    public String getUsername() {
        return this.username;
    }

    public void setUsername(String name) {
        this.username = name;
    }

    public String getPassword() {
        return this.password;
    }

    public void setPassword(password) {
        this.password = password;
    }

}
```

Notice that, for each property entity in the Spring XML configuration, we have a corresponding getter and setter defined in the Java class. In Spring terms, this is called *setter injection*, since the property values are configured by invoking the JavaBean's setter methods.

Constructor-Based Dependency Injection

An alternate approach is to use *constructor injection*, which allows the property values to be injected via the constructor of the class. To use constructor injection, we refactor our code and Spring configuration as follows:

```
<?xml version="1.0" encoding="UTF-8"?>
<beans xmlns=http://www.springframework.org/schema/beans
       xmlns:xsi=http://www.w3.org/2001/XMLSchema-instance
       xsi:schemaLocation="http://www.springframework.org/schema/beans
            http://www.springframework.org/schema/beans/spring-beans-4.1.xsd">

    <bean id="userBean" class="com.apress.springpersistence.audiomanager.core.domain.User">
        <constructor-arg index="0" value="admin" />
        <constructor-arg index="1" value="password" />
    </bean>

</beans>
```

And here's the corresponding code for the updated User bean:

```
package com.apress.springpersistence.audiomanager.core.domain;

public class User implements Serializable {

    private String username;
    private String password;

    public User(String username, String password) {
        this.username = username;
        this.password = password;
    }

    public String getUsername() {
        return this.username;
    }

    public String getPassword() {
        return this.password;
    }

}
```

Although either approach is valid, we recommend the setter-based approach, as this better conforms to the conventions of JavaBeans and makes your code easier to test later.

Instance Collaboration

In the preceding examples, we injected two string values, which are specified directly within the configuration file. This is a useful shortcut to abstract basic configuration details away from your code and into a more readily changeable file. However, the same concept can be taken a step further for satisfying dependencies between collaborating instances within your application.

For example, let's assume that authentication was implemented in a separate class. In our Spring configuration file, we might have the following:

```
<?xml version="1.0" encoding="UTF-8"?>
<beans xmlns=http://www.springframework.org/schema/beans
       xmlns:xsi=http://www.w3.org/2001/XMLSchema-instance
       xsi:schemaLocation="http://www.springframework.org/schema/beans
           http://www.springframework.org/schema/beans/spring-beans-4.1.xsd">

    <bean id="userBean" class="com.apress.springpersistence.audiomanager.core.domain.User">
        <property name="authHandler" ref="authService" />
    </bean>

    <bean id="authService" class="com.apress.springpersistence.audiomanager.core.service.
    impl.AuthServiceImpl"/>

</beans>
```

And here's the corresponding code for the updated User bean:

```
package com.apress.springpersistence.audiomanager.core.domain;

public class User implements Serializable {

    private AuthenticationService authHandler;

    public User() {
    }

    public AuthenticationService getAuthHandler() {
        return this.authHandler;
    }

    public void setAuthHandler(AuthenticationService authHandler) {
        this.authHandler = authHandler;
    }

}
```

Simple, isn't it? We just wired up critical parts of our application with a few configuration lines. It's easy to imagine defining code for an alternate authentication service and then simply modifying the bean reference in your Spring configuration to manipulate the behavior of your application.

Coding to Interfaces

Earlier, we mentioned that Spring has the tendency to lead developers to write better, cleaner, and more loosely coupled code. You might be starting to pick up on why this is the case. Not only are your classes free of application wiring code, but you'll also find that applications based on Spring are usually more interface-based, meaning that your code is dependent on interfaces rather than specific implementations. This strategy is often called *coding to interfaces*, which allows you to easily swap out one implementation for another simply by altering the class attribute within a Spring bean. As long as your code is written to rely on an interface, and the interface isn't changing, no changes to your class files will be necessary.

For instance, notice that in the preceding example, the User bean depends on an AuthenticationService bean. In your code, a good practice is to define an AuthenticationService interface that specifies core methods related to user access and security. Your code would then reference the AuthenticationService interface, and your Spring configuration would map the concrete implementation class to your User object.

As an oversimplified example, our AuthenticationService interface might look like the following:

```
package com.apress.springpersistence.audiomanager.core.service;

public interface AuthenticationService {
    public User authenticateUser(String username, String password)
      throws AuthenticationException;
}
```

And our concrete implementation would be something like this:

```
package com.apress.springpersistence.audiomanager.core.service.impl;

import com.apress.springpersistence.audiomanager.core.service.AuthenticationService;

public class AuthenticationServiceImpl implements AuthenticationService {

    public User authenticateUser(String username, String password)
      throws AuthenticationException {
        // authentication logic goes here
    }

}
```

Finally, bringing everything together in our Spring configuration, the userBean then points to a particular implementation of the AuthenticationService interface by using the ref property.

```
<?xml version="1.0" encoding="UTF-8"?>
<beans xmlns=http://www.springframework.org/schema/beans
       xmlns:xsi=http://www.w3.org/2001/XMLSchema-instance
       xsi:schemaLocation="http://www.springframework.org/schema/beans
            http://www.springframework.org/schema/beans/spring-beans-4.1.xsd">

    <bean id="userBean" class="com.apress.springpersistence.audiomanager.core.domain.User">
        <property name="authHandler" ref="authService" />
    </bean>

    <bean id="authService" class="com.apress.springpersistence.audiomanager.core.service.
    impl.AuthServiceImpl"/>

</beans>
```

The key point here is that the User class does not depend directly on the AuthenticationServiceImpl implementation, but rather on the AuthenticationService interface. Although the difference may appear subtle, expressing dependencies on interfaces is an effective means of ensuring your application is loosely coupled. If your code doesn't express any direct coupling to a particular implementation, you will gain the flexibility of defining these details in the Spring configuration, and only in that configuration. In this way, you can easily swap implementations without needing to refactor your code.

No matter what type of library, class, or framework you need to integrate into your application, Spring allows you to work with these internal and external components cleanly and with a shallow learning curve. This integration without direct coupling is the greatest benefit of IoC. Essentially, the hooks into third-party libraries (or even in-house frameworks and classes) are moved outside the source code and into configuration files (or annotation-based metadata within your classes). This type of configuration lets developers worry less about how the various components of code fit together and focus more on coding the core functionality itself.

Dependency Injection via Autowiring

Another type of injection is what Spring calls *autowiring*. This method allows you to simply define getters and setters of a particular type or name, putting on the Spring container the onus of figuring out which class to inject. This very powerful feature comes with some risk as well: should there be some ambiguity as to which instance to inject, you may run into problems. For instance, if you have a class that depends on the `AuthenticationService` interface and you have a `BasicAuthenticationServiceImpl` and a `RemoteAuthenticationServiceImpl` defined in your application (both of which implement the `AuthenticationService` interface), Spring may get confused as to which implementation you intend to inject.

Code-Based Dependency Injection

Up to this point, we've shown how to specify how objects depend on one another in XML configuration files. Over time, XML configurations for enterprise applications grew massive and unwieldy. Beginning with Spring 2.5 and JDK 1.5, another configuration strategy was introduced. Utilizing annotation-based metadata, you can now specify dependency wiring directly within your code. The advantage of this approach is that a class's dependencies can now benefit from the flexibility and type-safety afforded by Java. The downside is that you don't benefit from having a centralized collection of configuration files that illustrate and document how your application's components are wired.

Which path you take is up to you. Certainly, using annotations does simplify the configuration process. Furthermore, you can mix and match both XML configuration and annotations, allowing some aspects of your application to be configured within the Spring XML, while other details are wired via Java-based configuration and annotations.

There are several core features behind code-based Spring configuration. First off, a capability called *component scanning* allows Spring to search for Java classes (typically within a particular package) that have been annotated as Spring-managed beans. These "autodetected" classes often are annotated with `@Component` or one of its specialized annotations, such as `@Repository` or `@Service` (which typically indicate a class provides data access or service-level functionality, respectively). Once appropriately annotated classes have been discovered, they can be automatically wired into collaborating dependencies— utilizing the autowiring strategies described earlier. Throughout this book, you will see examples in which component scanning is used to discover and then autowire repository classes into service classes, providing a simpler alternative to the more explicit XML-based configuration.

In addition to autodetecting core classes within an application, component scanning can also detect `@Configuration` classes. These classes don't implement application business logic; instead, they offer the same type of XML-based Spring configuration that we reviewed earlier.

Configuration classes usually contain methods annotated with `@Bean` (as well as other configuration-specific annotations) annotations. Each method annotated with `@Bean` offers the same sort of functionality provided by an XML `<bean>` stanza. We won't go into too much detail just yet, but the short of it is that `@Bean` methods return (often preconfigured) instances of managed Spring beans, in much the same way that an XML-based configuration might specify a class attribute referencing a particular class to be instantiated by Spring, along with nested `<property>` elements defining references and values to inject to the managed bean that Spring intends to instantiate.

Let's look at an example of an entirely code-based configuration strategy that leverages autowiring, component scanning, and `@Configuration`.

```
import org.springframework.beans.factory.annotation.Autowired;
import org.springframework.stereotype.Service;

@Configuration
        @PropertySource("classpath:application.properties")
```

```
@ComponentScan(basePackages = {"com.apress.springpersistence.audiomanager"})
public class AppConfig {

@Value("${datasource.username}")
private String username;

@Value("${datasource.password}")
private String password;

@Bean
public DataSource dataSource() {
    DataSource ds =  new org.apache.commons.dbcp.BasicDataSource();
        ds.setUsername(this.username);
            ds.setPassword(this.password);
    ... other properties omitted . . .
    return ds;
}
        @Bean
        public AuthenticationService authenticationService() {
                AuthenticationService as = new AuthenticationServiceImpl();
                as.setDataSource(this.dataSource());
}

}

package com.apress.springpersistence.audiomanager.core.service.impl;

import com.apress.springpersistence.audiomanager.core.service.AuthenticationService;

        @Service
public class AuthenticationServiceImpl implements AuthenticationService {

        private DataSource dataSource;

        public DataSource getDataSource() {
                return this.dataSource;
        }

        public void setDataSource(DataSource ds) {
                this.dataSource = ds;
        }

        public User authenticateUser(String username, String password)
        throws AuthenticationException {
        // authentication logic goes here, using the injected DataSource
        }

}
```

In this (somewhat contrived) example, you see the use of two @Bean-configured methods. We have effectively created two managed Spring beans here: our AuthenticationService implementation, as well as a configured DataSource. As you will see next, you don't necessarily need to explicitly inject the DataSource directly into the AuthenticationService implementation (like earlier), but it's important to highlight that @Bean-annotated methods have the ability to do the same sorts of things that XML configuration can do (including importing other configuration classes, or even XML-based configuration resources).

Also note the use of @ComponentScan and @PropertySource (annotating the Configuration class). @ComponentScan tells Spring to look for other classes within the com.apress.springpersistence. audiomanager package that have been annotated with @Component or any of its derivatives. This includes other @Configuration classes or Spring-managed beans that provide application functionality.

The @PropertySource annotation tells the Configuration class to load a properties file, which is used to inject externalized values that you use for setting important properties of the DataSource. These externalized values can be injected via the @Value annotation, in which you specify an expression that can reference one of these externalized properties. You will learn more about how to use external properties files (and how these details can be encapsulated into the concept of an environment—an important Spring abstraction for managing application settings) later in this book.

Next, let's look at how you can autowire our AuthenticationService Spring bean into the User class discussed earlier.

```
'package com.apress.springpersistence.audiomanager.core.domain;

import org.springframework.beans.factory.annotation.Autowired;

public class User implements Serializable {

    @Autowired
    private AuthenticationService authHandler;

    public User() {
    }

    public AuthenticationService getAuthHandler() {
        return this.authHandler;
    }

    public void setAuthHandler(AuthenticationService authHandler) {
        this.authHandler = authHandler;
    }

}
```

This example shows how natural code-based configuration can be. You are able to express powerful metadata by simply annotating classes, properties, and methods. Additionally, you are able to describe application dependencies extremely naturally by using Java code.

Notice also that the @Autowired annotation above the authHandler member variable. This tells Spring to inject (using the autowiring strategy discussed earlier) an implementation of the AuthenticationService interface.

In cases where ambiguity could be an issue, Spring provides clues to the container by using qualifiers. *Qualifiers* can be inserted as a separate annotation on an @Autowired field or within an XML configuration to provide specific hints to the Spring container to disambiguate a situation in which multiple instances of a particular type or interface are present. For instance, you might indicate which AuthenticationService was needed by adding the following annotation:

```
@Autowired
@Qualifier("basicAuthHandler")
public void setAuthHandler(AuthenticationService authHandler) {
    this.authHandler = authHandler;
}
```

Now that you have disambiguated which implementation of our AuthenticationService should be injected into the setAuthHandler method, you need to "tag" this dependency so that Spring is able to select the correct instance. In Spring XML, you can provide this hint by including the following qualifier element:

```
<bean id="authHandler" class="com.prospringhibernate.gallery.BasicAuthServiceImpl"/>
    <qualifier value="basicAuthHandler"/>
</bean>
```

It is also possible to provide disambiguating hints on dependencies by applying the @Qualifier annotation to a class annotated for Spring's component-scanning capability. We will demonstrate these features later in this book. The @Autowired annotation may be applied to more than just member variables. It can also be applied to methods and constructors. Furthermore, the @Qualifier annotation may be applied directly to method parameters to target qualification to a specific parameter or to apply qualifying hints to parameters within a method or constructor.

Set It and Forget It!

All of this externalization doesn't seem like a big deal at first, but it really is, and you'll notice that when you begin development. You can simply focus on the implementation without worrying about how a reference from one class can get to another. You learn to simply define setters and getters for the dependencies each class requires, and then leave the wiring to Spring. Imagine some of the alternatives.

Many applications rely on singletons to centralize and hand out references to needed dependencies. This type of strategy will certainly work, but inevitably, your code becomes more about wiring classes together than about your application's core functionality.

Spring and IoC allow you to focus on the application design and business logic, and to forget about the wiring. Ron "Ronco" Popeil used the tagline "Set it and forget it!" in an infomercial. You may find this slogan floating through your head each time you begin developing with Spring.

Slick configuration and life-cycle management are only a small portion of the overall Spring package. Spring also provides powerful integration points to most major frameworks in the Java ecosystem, including many persistence frameworks. This greatly simplifies integrating these frameworks into an application and makes maintenance and development easier overall. Beyond these integration points, Spring also provides a powerful set of AOP and proxying features that are instrumental for configuring declarative transactions, logging, and remoting. These capabilities make Spring a viable replacement for the enterprise-level features offered by EJB and Java EE application servers.

Injecting Code Using AOP and Interceptors

AOP is often a hard pill for developers to swallow. In truth, it can be a somewhat confusing topic, as it is a fairly new development paradigm. For those experienced in object-oriented methodologies, AOP can seem a bit unconventional.

AOP is a strategy that allows behavior to be injected into code in places across an application. In much the same way that Spring provides a means to inject values and instance references into a bean, AOP allows developers to weave code from one class directly into another. Why on Earth would you ever want to do this? Well, sometimes, you want to apply functionality across a whole slew of classes, but extending from a base class to accomplish this goal doesn't make sense, as the functionality you wish to inject may be orthogonal to the destination class. This notion is often called *crosscutting concerns*, because the intention with AOP is to apply functionality across a series of classes that has little to do with the main purposes of those classes.

For example, let's say that you have a few classes that are designed to store and retrieve data to and from a relational database. As part of this implementation, you may wish to do some auditing (for example, to track details of each successive write operation). Extending from a base auditing class isn't a viable or proper way to accomplish this task. If you extend from any class at all, you probably want to inherit behavior that relates more to manipulating your domain model and saving data (you don't want to inherit auditing behavior). In this example, you might say that auditing functionality is *orthogonal* to the core persistence functionality (that is, completely independent of it). Furthermore, the auditing aspects of the code can be applied in a reasonably similar and standard fashion across all the application code. This is the perfect scenario for AOP. You can apply aspects of the unrelated auditing functionality across all of the classes that aim to handle image gallery logic.

The way AOP works in practice is fairly simple: a class's methods can be altered so that new functionality can be injected before, after, or around (essentially, before *and* after) a method is called. So, in the case of an auditing aspect, you could inject a block of code that writes a row in a database (constituting a piece of an overall auditing trail) each time a method within a category of methods is called.

A similar scenario concerns security. A security check can be inserted into your core data access code to ensure appropriate permissions or roles are verified each time certain methods are called. The interesting part of this approach is that you can keep the security code entirely separate from your core implementation (which no longer needs to worry about the implementation details of security). This leads to cleaner code, as your core application need not get bogged down with details of your security implementation.

Furthermore, it is often useful to have distinct teams manage features that are disparate. AOP makes this feasible, as security-related code can be crafted by experts in this domain, while the application business logic is developed and maintained by a different team. By ensuring these two facets don't intermingle (from a code standpoint), specialization becomes more attainable. These two distinct pieces of functionality can be developed and maintained entirely separately, leading to cleaner and more loosely coupled code.

This ability to intercept method calls and introduce, or *inject*, new functionality is the secret sauce behind Spring's support for declarative transactions. Using Spring's declarative transaction support, you can advise your persistence facade layer with transactional semantics. We'll cover transactions in detail in Chapter 7, but to illustrate the separation of concerns offered by AOP, we'll leave you with this snippet of code as a teaser:

```
public class ServiceFacadeImpl implements ServiceFacade {

    @Transactional(readOnly = false, propagation = Propagation.REQUIRES_NEW)
    public void save(Map map) {
        // business logic goes here
    }

}
```

By simply annotating this method as @Transactional, Spring can enforce the transaction semantics specified, without requiring that you write any code to start and complete a transaction in the body of the save method. Don't worry about the details associated with the annotation for now. Just know that externalizing this logic via AOP enables modifications to the transaction implementation without requiring you to refactor all the portions of the code base that depend on it. Similarly, you can be confident that changes to the core business logic won't break the transaction semantics.

Summary

In this chapter, you've learned about the fundamental concepts that power the Spring Framework. You saw how to bootstrap a Spring ApplicationContext, learned the basics of configuring bean dependencies in Spring XML configuration files, and developed an understanding of bean scopes and life cycles. The benefits of dependency injection are now clear. You can effectively delegate to the Spring container to manage and resolve your application dependencies, and doing so can help keep your application's dependencies loosely coupled. Finally, you were given a glimpse into the power of managing orthogonal coding concerns with AOP.

Throughout the rest of this book, we will build on the Spring concepts introduced in this chapter to define and implement an art gallery application.

CHAPTER 3

Basic Application Setup

In this chapter, we'll take you on a crash course though setting up a basic project using Spring and Hibernate. The tool we'll use for managing our application is Apache Maven 3. If you're already well versed in Spring, Hibernate, and Maven, you may want to just skim through this chapter, so you can get a feel for the structure and conventions we'll be using throughout the book as we flesh out our media manager application. We're going to cover a lot of ground very quickly and provide references to the chapters where we dive deeper into the various configurations along the way.

Application Management with Maven

Maven was written by Sonatype's Jason van Zyl in 2002. It reached its 1.0 release as a top-level Apache Software Foundation project in 2004. Maven strives to simplify day-to-day development by ensuring an easy, repeatable process for configuring, managing, and interacting with Java-based software projects.

Maven revolves around the concept of a Project Object Model (POM), which represents the configuration for your project or module. In Maven parlance, a module is a subproject for a given "parent" Maven project. This organizational construct allows you to create a project that is compartmentalized into a collection of smaller modules. Your POM describes many things about your project, including required dependencies, plugin configuration, and the order and operations for compiling and assembling your application. Defining a model for encapsulating the metadata related to building and distributing a project (as well as managing its dependencies) facilitates a standardized build process that is inherently extensible and well understood.

Contrast this approach with procedural build systems, such as Ant and Make, which require developers to decipher and manage low-level tasks responsible for handling the drudgery of locating and manipulating files, compiling code, and distributing artifacts. Most projects share the same essential characteristics and structure (or at least they should, if adhering to best practices and conventions). So there's not much point in managing a project's build process through a collection of tasks when you can define your project's structure through standardized metadata, which then allow you to leverage Maven's build life cycle and take advantage of numerous Maven plugins.

Maven provides a ton of out-of-the-box features. Additionally, a large number of Maven plugins have been developed by its massive community of users. When the time comes to further customize your project's build process, writing Maven plugins on your own is a snap.

Managed Dependencies

Maven's killer feature is its dependency management. Maven downloads all of your project's dependencies from Maven repositories when you build or compile your application. This is a huge win when working in a team. Do you want to upgrade the version of Spring your project uses? Just update the dependencies section of your POM XML file, commit to source control, and everyone on the team will automatically have their project upgraded to the newest version of Spring as well (once they run the appropriate Maven command,

© Paul Fisher and Brian D. Murphy 2016
P. Fisher and B.D. Murphy, *Spring Persistence with Hibernate*, DOI 10.1007/978-1-4842-0268-5_3

of course)! Maven even handles transitive dependencies, meaning that Maven can automatically fetch the dependencies of the libraries upon which your project depends, without having to explicitly include them all. Again, these features are all enabled through Maven's approach of declaratively defining your project's structure and metadata, rather than scripting the procedural tasks for handling the much repeated steps of building and compiling your application.

Remember how we told you that there are a huge number of mature plugins available for Maven? One example of a handy plugin that you have at your disposal is the excellent M2Eclipse plugin, for integrating Maven with Eclipse. Figure 3-1, which comes courtesy of M2Eclipse, shows you everything you need to know about why using a tool like Maven is important for managing enterprise Java applications. The image isn't very legible: you can't even see all of the dependencies, which extend off to the left and right of the screen, because there are so many components that make up our application.

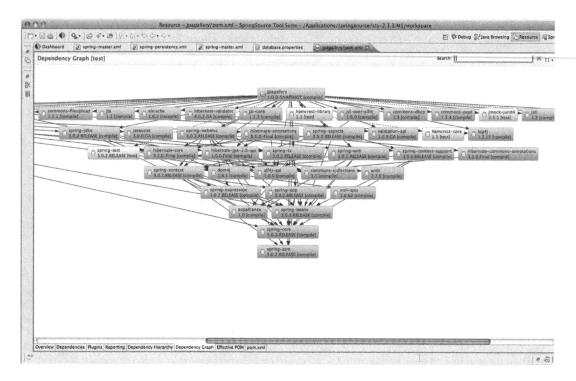

Figure 3-1. *A set of dependencies as displayed by Maven and M2Eclipse*

If you are using a different IDE, such as JetBrains IntelliJ, you can directly import a Maven project, and many of Maven's features are natively integrated into the IDE as well.

The number of dependencies may seem a bit daunting at first, but when you're using Spring and Hibernate, you are given a lot of granular choices about which JARs to include and when, which to exclude, and so on. This results in many smaller library dependencies. Through your project's dependency configuration, Maven is aware of which JAR files are required for your project and which JARs have dependencies on one another. It knows which libraries are needed only for the purpose of executing unit tests, as well as which libraries should be bundled into your resulting WAR file to be deployed on an application server like Apache Tomcat.

With all of this power comes a good bit of complexity, and for that reason, Maven also has its fair share of detractors. The fact remains that at the time of this writing, Maven is far and away the most prevalent tool used by shops big and small for managing Java applications. Once you get over some of the jargon, Maven is quite simple to configure and use. Get started by downloading it from `http://maven.apache.org`. Let's see how we can put it to use.

Standard Directory Structure

Let's first create the folder structure required for a standard Maven 3 web application. Though you can define a custom directory structure and modify your Maven settings (or graft Maven onto a legacy project with a directory structure that's already defined), your best bet is to stick with the basic folder structure that Maven expects (and is a well-regarded convention). This also ensures proper interoperability with all of the plugins and tools that are available.

Since we're building a Media Management API, start by making a folder called `mediaApi`:

```
mkdir mediaApi
```

Within the `mediaApi` folder, we'll create the folders that are customary for a Java application:

```
mkdir -p gallery/src/main/java
mkdir -p gallery/src/main/resources/META-INF
```

For web applications, we need a `webapp` and `WEB-INF` folder:

```
mkdir -p gallery/src/main/webapp/WEB-INF
```

We also need to create the folders that are required for unit testing our application:

```
mkdir -p gallery/src/test/java
mkdir gallery/src/test/resources
```

And finally, we'll create the two folders where Spring configuration files are ordinarily placed:

```
mkdir gallery/src/main/webapp/WEB-INF/spring
mkdir gallery/src/main/resources/META-INF/spring
```

■ **Note**   Maven can automatically generate your project's structure by using Maven's archetype feature. Maven archetypes are like project templates that can be used to streamline the creation of a Maven project, including setting up your directory structure and a baseline `pom.xml` file.

POM Deconstruction

The primary configuration file for Maven is `pom.xml`. With this configuration file, you can specify important metadata and build details about your project. The `pom.xml` file resides at the root of a given Maven project, so we'll create it within the `gallery` folder. This listing is abridged for the sake of simplicity. We recommend you check out the full listing in the source code that accompanies the book.

```xml
<?xml version="1.0" encoding="UTF-8"?>
<project xmlns="http://maven.apache.org/POM/4.0.0"
         xmlns:xsi="http://www.w3.org/2001/XMLSchema-instance"
         xsi:schemaLocation="http://maven.apache.org/POM/4.0.0
         http://maven.apache.org/xsd/maven-4.0.0.xsd">

    <modelVersion>4.0.0</modelVersion>

    <parent>
        <groupId>org.springframework.boot</groupId>
        <artifactId>spring-boot-starter-parent</artifactId>
        <version>1.2.2.RELEASE</version>
    </parent>

    <groupId>com.apress.springpersistence</groupId>
    <artifactId>audio-manager</artifactId>
    <name>Spring Persistence Sample Application</name>
    <description>Spring Persistence Sample Application</description>
    <version>0.1.0</version>

    <properties>
        <java.version>1.8</java.version>
        <jetty.version>9.2.10.v20150310</jetty.version>
        <project.build.sourceEncoding>UTF-8</project.build.sourceEncoding>
        <project.reporting.outputEncoding>UTF-8</project.reporting.outputEncoding>
        <flyway.version>3.0</flyway.version>
        <db.username>sa</db.username>
        <db.password>test</db.password>
        <db.host>localhost</db.host>
        <db.db>audiomanager</db.db>
        <db.port>5432</db.port>
    </properties>

    <dependencies>
        <dependency>
            <groupId>org.springframework.boot</groupId>
            <artifactId>spring-boot-starter-data-rest</artifactId>
        </dependency>
        <dependency>
            <groupId>org.springframework.boot</groupId>
            <artifactId>spring-boot-starter-data-jpa</artifactId>
        </dependency>
        <dependency>
            <groupId>com.h2database</groupId>
            <artifactId>h2</artifactId>
        </dependency>
        <dependency>
            <groupId>org.apache.derby</groupId>
            <artifactId>derby</artifactId>
            <version>10.11.1.1</version>
        </dependency>
```

```xml
    <dependency>
        <groupId>org.springframework.boot</groupId>
        <artifactId>spring-boot-starter-test</artifactId>
        <scope>test</scope>
    </dependency>
    <dependency>
        <groupId>com.jayway.restassured</groupId>
        <artifactId>spring-mock-mvc</artifactId>
        <version>2.4.1</version>
        <scope>test</scope>
    </dependency>
</dependencies>

<build>
    <plugins>
        <plugin>
            <groupId>org.springframework.boot</groupId>
            <artifactId>spring-boot-maven-plugin</artifactId>
            <dependencies>
                <dependency>
                    <groupId>org.springframework</groupId>
                    <artifactId>springloaded</artifactId>
                    <version>1.2.3.RELEASE</version>
                </dependency>
            </dependencies>
        </plugin>
        <plugin>
            <groupId>org.eclipse.jetty</groupId>
            <artifactId>jetty-maven-plugin</artifactId>
            <version>${jetty.version}</version>
        </plugin>

        <plugin>
            <groupId>org.flywaydb</groupId>
            <artifactId>flyway-maven-plugin</artifactId>
            <version>${flyway.version}</version>
            <configuration>
                <!--<url>jdbc:postgresql://${db.host}:${db.port}/${db.db}</url>-->
                <url>jdbc:derby:${db.db}</url>
                <driver>org.apache.derby.jdbc.EmbeddedDriver</driver>
                <user>${db.username}</user>
                <password>${db.password}</password>
                <schemas>
                    <schema>public</schema>
                </schemas>
                <locations>
                    <location>filesystem:${project.basedir}/src/main/sql/
                    migration</location>
                    <location>db/migration</location>
                </locations>
                <initVersion>1.0</initVersion>
```

```
                </configuration>
                <dependencies>
                    <dependency>
                        <groupId>org.apache.derby</groupId>
                        <artifactId>derby</artifactId>
                        <version>10.11.1.1</version>
                    </dependency>
                </dependencies>
            </plugin>

        </plugins>
    </build>

    <repositories>
        <repository>
            <id>spring-releases</id>
            <url>https://repo.spring.io/libs-release</url>
        </repository>
    </repositories>
    <pluginRepositories>
        <pluginRepository>
            <id>spring-releases</id>
            <url>https://repo.spring.io/libs-release</url>
        </pluginRepository>
    </pluginRepositories>

</project>
```

There is a lot happening in this POM configuration file. First, you'll notice the XML namespace that's defined for Maven and its POM schema definition.

modelVersion is used to declare the version of the POM for your project. This protects you from compatibility issues when upgrading the version of Maven that you are using.

Below the modelVersion, you will notice a parent entity, under which are nested group, version, and artifactId elements. The parent element is Maven's mechanism for implementing polymorphism, which is a great way to reuse and share configuration. In this case, we are extending from the Spring Boot's parent POM, which defines all of the core Spring Framework dependencies, as well as some useful Maven plugins that help streamline development and testing.

We will learn more about Spring Boot later in this chapter, but all you need to know for now is that the Spring Boot project helps to streamline project setup and configuration, significantly reducing the amount of boilerplate required to get a project up and running. This benefit comes with a small price, in terms of additional "autoconfiguration" magic that may obscure some of the lower-level implementation details and potentially create some debugging issues. However, we will examine closely what Spring Boot is doing behind the scenes, and also look at alternative configuration strategies that don't rely on this (very useful and powerful) project.

Next up is a series of fields commonly referred to as the *project coordinates* because they uniquely identify the project. By convention, the groupId uses the reverse domain of the organization that created the project. The artifactId is the unique name within a given groupId, and version is the specific release of a project. No two projects may have the same combination of groupId:artifactId:version.

The packaging element is a special attribute in the project coordinates. It's not used as a part of the unique identifier, but it describes the output of a given project. The default value is jar, to produce a Java archive (JAR file). Since, we're building a web application, we specify war to output a web archive (WAR file).

The properties section offers a convenient place to define variables that can be referenced in other parts of the project configuration. In our POM, we have defined several Spring dependencies (and many more implicitly defined through the parent POM). Managing the different versions of each project dependency can get somewhat tedious. By leveraging Maven properties, we can extract important attributes and dependency versions, decoupling and centralizing these details into the properties section of your POM, thereby simplifying the management (and upgrading) of project dependencies and plugins.

Finally, the build attribute offers a place for you to define, among other things, the plugins you require for your project. For our project, the Jetty Maven plugin provides an excellent mechanism for easily building and running our web application on the Jetty application server. The Maven Jetty plugin offers several useful features to simplify development and testing, but please keep in mind that it doesn't reduce web container portability — you can still deploy your web application to any other servlet container, such as Tomcat or Resin.

With that, we have a very basic application stubbed out. You can execute mvn initialize from the root of the project directory. If you've done everything correctly, Maven will fetch your dependencies, setup any necessary project structure, and deliver the message BUILD SUCCESS.

Of course, our application doesn't yet *do* anything. Let's start defining our Spring configuration so we can change that.

Spring Configuration

When building reasonably large Spring applications, you end up with a lot of Spring beans configured in the Spring ApplicationContext. As you saw in Chapter 2, every object that you configure for use in the Spring container is registered in the ApplicationContext, which is a subinterface of Spring's BeanFactory. The ApplicationContext provides you with the tools you need to interact with and leverage your configured beans.

There are several recommended approaches for configuring your Spring applications. In this book, we will examine two primary strategies: one that is driven by XML configuration and another that is entirely configured via Java configuration. Legacy applications will likely be predominantly XML-based, since Java configuration is a feature that came more recently. There are pros and cons to both strategies, so each method is given a thorough examination.

In this chapter, we will begin configuring our application using an approach that is driven primarily via XML configuration— a setup that you are more likely to find within older applications that predate the Java-based configuration strategy. In the following chapter, we will look at an alternative setup that leverages predominantly Java-based configuration—the more current and widely recommended approach. In order to get up and running more quickly, we are going to utilize Spring Boot, which offers several shortcuts in configuring our application.

The following class is the starting point for the application. It is annotated with the @Configuration annotation, which tells the Spring container that the methods inside the class define Spring beans, into which they can be injected in other container-managed dependencies. This is actually one of the key features of Java-based configuration, but we are still using it within our mostly XML-based approach in order to leverage Spring Boot.

```
package com.apress.springpersistence.audiomanager;

import org.springframework.boot.SpringApplication;
import org.springframework.boot.autoconfigure.EnableAutoConfiguration;
import org.springframework.context.annotation.*;
```

```
/**
 * Created by pfisher on 9/27/14.
 */
import org.springframework.boot.SpringApplication;
import org.springframework.boot.autoconfigure.EnableAutoConfiguration;
import org.springframework.context.annotation.ComponentScan;
import org.springframework.context.annotation.Configuration;
import org.springframework.data.jpa.repository.config.EnableJpaRepositories;
import org.springframework.data.rest.webmvc.config.RepositoryRestMvcConfiguration;

@Configuration
@EnableJpaRepositories
@Import(RepositoryRestMvcConfiguration.class)
@EnableAutoConfiguration
public class AudioManagerApplication {

    public static void main(String[] args) throws Exception {
        SpringApplication.run(AudioManagerApplication.class, args);
    }
}
```

Next, we have our core XML configuration file, called applicationContext-core.xml. We have located all of our Spring configuration files inside the src/main/resources/spring directory. The following listing contains the entirety of applicationContext-core.xml:

```
<?xml version="1.0" encoding="UTF-8" standalone="no"?>
<beans xmlns="http://www.springframework.org/schema/beans"
       xmlns:aop="http://www.springframework.org/schema/aop"
       xmlns:context="http://www.springframework.org/schema/context"
       xmlns:tx="http://www.springframework.org/schema/tx"
       xmlns:xsi="http://www.w3.org/2001/XMLSchema-instance"
       xsi:schemaLocation="http://www.springframework.org/schema/aop
       http://www.springframework.org/schema/aop/spring-aop-4.1.xsd
       http://www.springframework.org/schema/beans
       http://www.springframework.org/schema/beans/spring-beans-4.1.xsd
       http://www.springframework.org/schema/context
       http://www.springframework.org/schema/context/spring-context-4.1.xsd
       http://www.springframework.org/schema/tx
       http://www.springframework.org/schema/tx/spring-tx-4.1.xsd">
    <!--
        This will automatically locate any and all property files you have
        within your classpath, provided they fall under the META-INF/spring
        directory. The located property files are parsed and their values can
        then be used within application context files in the form of
        ${propertyKey}.
    -->
    <context:property-placeholder
            ignore-resource-not-found="true"
            location="classpath*:*.properties"/>
```

```xml
<!-- post-processors -->
<context:annotation-config/>

<context:spring-configured/>

<context:component-scan base-package="com.apress.springpersistence">
    <context:exclude-filter expression="org.springframework.stereotype.Controller"
    type="annotation"/>
</context:component-scan>
<bean class="org.apache.commons.dbcp.BasicDataSource" destroy-method="close"
id="dataSource">
    <property name="driverClassName" value="${jpa.driver.classname}"/>
    <property name="url" value="${database.url}"/>
    <property name="username" value="${database.username}"/>
    <property name="password" value="${database.password}"/>
    <property name="testOnBorrow" value="true"/>
    <property name="testOnReturn" value="true"/>
    <property name="testWhileIdle" value="true"/>
    <property name="timeBetweenEvictionRunsMillis" value="1800000"/>
    <property name="numTestsPerEvictionRun" value="3"/>
    <property name="minEvictableIdleTimeMillis" value="1800000"/>
    <property name="validationQuery" value="SELECT 1;"/>
</bean>

<!--Use Hibernate SessionFactory instead? -->
<bean class="org.springframework.orm.jpa.JpaTransactionManager" id="transactionManager">
    <property name="entityManagerFactory" ref="entityManagerFactory"/>
</bean>
<tx:annotation-driven />

<bean class="org.springframework.orm.jpa.LocalContainerEntityManagerFactoryBean"
id="entityManagerFactory">
    <property name="persistenceUnitName" value="persistenceUnit"/>
    <property name="dataSource" ref="dataSource"/>
    <property name="persistenceXmlLocation" value="classpath:META-INF/
    persistence.xml"></property>
    <property name="jpaDialect" value="${jpa.dialect}"/>
    <property name="packagesToScan" value="${jpa.entities.package}"/>
</bean>
```

```xml
</beans>
```

Let's break down the contents of this applicationContext-core.xml file in more detail.

Namespace Support

Spring introduced extensive namespace support as of version 2.0 of the framework. Everything is just a bean in the IoC container, but over time, your configuration can become incredibly verbose. The introduction of namespaces is intended to simplify the XML configuration when dealing with integration points like transactions. You can even define your own namespaces if that's required.

Three namespaces are used in our `applicationContext-core.xml` configuration file, marked by the `xmlns` declarations:

- The `beans` namespace is required for defining all basic bean definitions for your application (such as DAOs, service layer beans, and so on).

- The `context` namespace is provided as a convenience for configuring some of the core plumbing of Spring.

- The `tx` namespace offers a streamlined means of defining transactional behavior.

Externalizing Property Configurations

This configuration defines a `PropertyPlaceholderConfigurer`, which allows you to externalize some of your settings to a properties file outside the Spring configuration.

```
<context:property-placeholder
        ignore-resource-not-found="true"
        location="classpath*:*.properties"/>
```

The `property-placeholder` automatically locates and parses any property files that you have in the root of your classpath (or the location defined as the value of the location attribute). Any property that you want to replace should be indicated in your Spring configuration, like so: `${propertyKey}`. You'll see a full example later in this chapter when we configure a datasource for the media management application.

Component Scanning

The next important piece of configuration is *component scanning*, which was first introduced in Spring 2.5 as a mechanism to further simplify configuring Spring applications.

```
<context:component-scan base-package="com.apress.springpersistence">
    <context:exclude-filter expression="org.springframework.stereotype.Controller"
    type="annotation"/>
</context:component-scan>
```

This declaration will cause Spring to locate every `@Component`, `@Repository`, and `@Service` in your application. In practical terms, this allows you to write a POJO, and then simply annotate the new POJO as a `@Service`. Spring will then automatically detect, instantiate, and dependency inject your service at startup time.

Additionally, component scanning can be used to load any classes annotated with the `@Configuration` annotation. This is typically how Java-based Spring configuration is integrated into an application.

Furthermore, component scanning turns on other notable Spring annotations like `@Inject`, `@Named`, and `@PostConstruct` support. These annotations allow you to use common Spring and Java EE annotations in your classes without needing to do any special configuration. The most commonly used annotation is `@Inject`, which instructs Spring to dependency inject an object into your class. You can then also have your new service injected into any other class that requires it, simply by declaring a field for your service inside the relying class.

> ■ **Note** @Inject and @Named are just two of the annotations defined as a part of JSR-330. JSR-330 defines a standard set of annotations to be used in Java EE applications. @Inject and @Named are wholesale replacements for the @Autowired and @Qualifier annotations in Spring that you may already be familiar with. Using the JSR-330 annotations makes your application more portable in the event that you should decide to change your dependency injection implementation to something other than Spring.

The matching rules used by the component scanner can also be customized with filters for including or excluding components. You can control this matching based on type, annotation, AspectJ expression, or regular expressions for name patterns. The default stereotypes can even be disabled. In our configuration, we declared the following exclusion:

```
<context:exclude-filter type="annotation" expression="org.springframework.
stereotype.Controller" />
```

This exclude-filter is declared to avoid instantiating our @Controller classes, as these should be instantiated by a web tier application context. Yes, you read that right: our application will actually have several distinct application contexts. We will talk about this a bit more when we introduce our web application configuration via web.xml later in this chapter.

Import Statements

After the property-placeholder configurer, you'll notice that we specify an import statement:

```
<import resource="applicationContext-jpa.xml"/>
<import resource="applicationContext-web.xml"/>
```

Imports allow you to specify an external Spring configuration file to be integrated into your application context. This is a useful construct, especially in our demonstration application, as we can easily modularize the different persistence strategies, keeping each version in its own file. These imports can also reference your application classpath with the following syntax:

```
<import resource="classpath*:spring-config-name.xml"/>
```

Imports are invaluable when you're dealing with large application contexts, as they provide a great deal of flexibility for organizing your bean definitions. You can partition your application in any number of ways to make it more approachable by new developers and to help understand how the project changes over time.

Database Integration

Now that you have a clearer picture of how Spring is bootstrapped within your application, let's get back to integrating your database of choice. You've learned that Spring's adherence to interface-based concepts helps to take implementation choices out of your code and into configuration. So, whether you choose to use a Java Naming and Directory Interface (JNDI) factory bean to pull in a database reference from an external JNDI directory or configure a specific database driver directly, your code won't be affected one bit. In the end, you'll always end up with a JDBC DataSource, and that's all your code needs to care about.

JDBC Support

In our example, we'll keep things simple. Let's start by defining a Spring bean that creates a JDBC DataSource instance:

```
<bean class=" org.springframework.jdbc.datasource.DriverManagerDataSource " destroy-
method="close" id="mediaDataSource">
    <property name="driverClassName" value="${jpa.driver.classname}"/>
    <property name="url" value="${database.url}"/>
    <property name="username" value="${database.username}"/>
    <property name="password" value="${database.password}"/>
    <property name="testOnBorrow" value="true"/>
    <property name="testOnReturn" value="true"/>
    <property name="testWhileIdle" value="true"/>
    <property name="timeBetweenEvictionRunsMillis" value="1800000"/>
    <property name="numTestsPerEvictionRun" value="3"/>
    <property name="minEvictableIdleTimeMillis" value="1800000"/>
    <property name="validationQuery" value="SELECT 1;"/>
</bean>
```

You will note that we are using a class called `DriverManagerDataSource`— this implementation provided by Spring is useful for development or testing purposes, but we would probably want to utilize a popular database connection pool as our bean implementation when running our application in a Production environment. A connection pool is ideal for web applications that require multiple concurrent database operations. A connection pool can be optimized for different usage scenarios, ensuring a more efficient means for handing off new database connections to the application. Again, switching to a database connection pool will give your application more efficiency without requiring any code change.

■ **Note**   Connection pools used to be something that developers had to write on their own. Their use is actually a fun gauge to use to see how long engineers have been writing web applications in Java. If they've written their own connection pools, they've probably been at it for a long while. As a result of needing to roll their own pools, every open source project wound up with a unique implementation of a connection pool. Fortunately, all of the projects that are part of the Apache Software Foundation came together to create the `commons-dbcp` library (dbcp is short for database connection pool).

In the following configuration, note how easily we switch to using a connection pool. This is made possible by coding to interfaces, externalizing configuration, and leveraging dependency injection. It's a really rewarding experience to be able to make such large changes so quickly and easily.

```
<bean class="org.apache.commons.dbcp.BasicDataSource" destroy-method="close"
id="mediaDataSource">
    <property name="driverClassName" value="${jpa.driver.classname}"/>
    <property name="url" value="${database.url}"/>
    <property name="username" value="${database.username}"/>
    <property name="password" value="${database.password}"/>
    <property name="testOnBorrow" value="true"/>
    <property name="testOnReturn" value="true"/>
    <property name="testWhileIdle" value="true"/>
```

```
        <property name="timeBetweenEvictionRunsMillis" value="1800000"/>
        <property name="numTestsPerEvictionRun" value="3"/>
        <property name="minEvictableIdleTimeMillis" value="1800000"/>
        <property name="validationQuery" value="SELECT 1;"/>
</bean>
```

You may have noticed that the id for our DataSource bean is mediaDataSource. In many enterprise applications, you end up with several datasources. As a result, the best approach is to give each one a unique name so you have finer-grained control over which portions of your application use which datasource.

Also notice that we have specified properties for driverClassName, url, username, and password for our datasource bean. These properties determine how an application connects to a given database. Within the Spring configuration, we can use placeholder references through the ${} notation. These placeholders represent external values stored in our jdbc.properties file, injected into our configuration file, courtesy of our PropertyPlaceholderConfigurer. This detail isn't necessary, but it makes our configuration more portable. It allows us to easily define different database configurations for different machines and platforms without needing to change our Spring configuration. For instance, here is a snippet of our src/main/resources/META-INF/spring/jpa-dev.properties file:

```
jpa.db.name=derbydb
jpa.db.create.strategy=create
jpa.hibernate.create.strategy=create-drop
jpa.dialect=org.hibernate.dialect.DerbyTenSevenDialect
jpa.entities.package=com.apress.springpersistence.audiomanager.core.domain
database.username=sa
database.password=test
jpa.unique.resource.name=audiomanager
jpa.driver.classname=org.apache.derby.jdbc.EmbeddedDriver
```

The syntax is intuitive. Each line contains a simple expression, in which the left side represents the property name and the right side (after the =) represents the configured value. This externalization makes it easy to swap different database configurations for different environments and better externalizes these details from application-specific configuration.

Different databases will require different JDBC URLs. In this example, we use the popular Derby database. Derby is a Java-based database and is therefore easy to integrate into any Java-based application (it doesn't require a separate database process). You could just as easily use PostgreSQL, MySQL, or any database for which a JDBC driver is available. Just make sure your database is up, running, and configured to listen on the URL specified in the bean's configuration.

It is also critical that you include the appropriate JDBC driver on your classpath when the application is first started. Because Derby is Java-based, simply including the Derby JAR file on your classpath is all that is required to get rolling.

Integration with JNDI

Hibernate almost always implies a relational database, so starting there makes the most sense. Java has evolved into a platform for building enterprise-level applications, so there are many options for connecting it to a standard relational database.

At the simplest level, you can instantiate the database driver for your database of choice, but most applications require more than that. Many application servers offer their own optimized database connection pools to improve performance when multiple clients are using the application concurrently. To simplify administration and integration, many application servers use JNDI to interface with a database.

JNDI is often described as the opposite of Spring's IoC. Instead of having dependencies automatically injected into your application, JNDI allows dependencies to be looked up from a centrally managed directory. There are certainly benefits to both approaches. For example, in the case of JNDI, developers can define logical names for database resources in their application configuration, but allow a system administrator to manage mapping that logical name to the proper database connection pool in the web application container configurations, effectively deferring the specification of database connection details until runtime. When a database migration is required, JNDI can simplify some of these administrative tasks, as no changes to the application configuration will be required.

No matter which approach you decide to take, Spring makes integrating a datasource into your application easy. The key factor is that Spring's persistence templates never require a specific type of datasource implementation. Instead, they depend on the more generic javax.sql.Datasource interface. Whether you intend to use a database connection pool or a JNDI-retrieved datasource, the resultant configuration should always produce a standard javax.sql.Datasource reference.

This brings us to a key concept in Spring: the FactoryBean interface. The FactoryBean is Spring's answer to the well-known factory design pattern. The key concept here is that you remove a direct dependency on a specific implementation by delaying the selection or instantiation of the specific implementation until runtime. You define a factory, and it is the factory's job to pick the correct implementation at runtime and instantiate (or look up) that specific class.

The Spring FactoryBean concept is quite similar. Normally in Spring, when you define a bean, the class specified by the classname attribute is the class that will be instantiated and injected into other beans that have that bean ID wired into them. This isn't the case with a FactoryBean. When you use a FactoryBean, you are instead instantiating a factory class that will then be responsible for creating the specific implementation used to resolve dependencies in Spring. So essentially, the classname attribute in this case just defines a factory implementation, whose job will then be to create the actual target implementation you need.

This concept allows us to use multiple strategies to access a datasource without tying ourselves down to a particular solution. If you use the JNDI FactoryBean, you will still end up with a datasource reference, and the same will occur if you choose to use the pooled datasource implementation.

There are other reasons to use a FactoryBean in Spring, as well. For instance, a MapFactoryBean can be used to create a Java Map entirely in your configuration file (which is quite convenient in certain cases).

A Spring FactoryBean implements the FactoryBean interface, which defines three methods designed to instantiate the target object (i.e., the instance that the factory intends to create), the target object's type, and whether the target object is a singleton or prototype. For our scenario, we would configure our JNDI datasource as follows:

```
<bean id="mediaDatasource" class="org.springframework.jndi.JndiObjectFactoryBean">
    <property name="jndiName" value="java:comp/env/jdbc/audioDS"/>
</bean>
```

Although the preceding example is fairly concise, in some situations, you can make your configuration terser and easier to read by importing a namespace intended to handle a very specific type of configuration. For example, by importing the jee namespace, we can simplify the preceding JNDI lookup further:

```
<jee:jndi-lookup id="audioyDatasource"
        jndi-name="java:comp/env/jdbc/audioDS"/>
```

Not only have we reduced the configuration to a single line, but we've also made the intention of our configuration clearer.

Web Application Configuration

Java web applications are deployed as WAR files. A WAR file is a special kind of JAR file that includes things like servlets, JSPs, tag libraries, and static HTML assets.

The key configuration file for a WAR is web.xml, which outlines the structure for an application in accordance with the Java EE specifications. The configuration that follows adheres to the Servlet 3.0 specification, and can be interpreted by all major application server containers, including Tomcat, Resin, Jetty, WebSphere, WebLogic, GlassFish, and so on. The web.xml file should be placed under the WEB-INF directory. For Maven projects, the WEB-INF directory is located under src/main/webapp. Here's a basic src/main/webapp/WEB-INF/web.xml to get our media manager application started.

```xml
<?xml version="1.0" encoding="UTF-8" standalone="no"?>
<web-app xmlns:xsi="http://www.w3.org/2001/XMLSchema-instance"
        xmlns="http://java.sun.com/xml/ns/javaee"
        xmlns:web="http://java.sun.com/xml/ns/javaee/web-app_3_0.xsd"
        xsi:schemaLocation="http://java.sun.com/xml/ns/javaee http://java.sun.com/xml/ns/
        javaee/web-app_3_0.xsd"
        version="3.0">

<display-name>media-manager-web</display-name>

<context-param>
    <param-name>log4jConfigLocation</param-name>
    <param-value>file:${ext.properties.dir:${user.home}/.hc}/helix-console.log4j.
    properties</param-value>
</context-param>
<context-param>
    <param-name>log4jExposeWebAppRoot</param-name>
    <param-value>false</param-value>
</context-param>

<context-param>
    <param-name>contextConfigLocation</param-name>
    <param-value>classpath*:spring/applicationContext*.xml</param-value>
</context-param>
<filter>
    <filter-name>CharacterEncodingFilter</filter-name>
    <filter-class>org.springframework.web.filter.CharacterEncodingFilter</filter-class>
     <init-param>
        <param-name>encoding</param-name>
        <param-value>UTF-8</param-value>
    </init-param>
    <init-param>
        <param-name>forceEncoding</param-name>
        <param-value>true</param-value>
    </init-param>
</filter>

<filter>
    <filter-name>springSecurityFilterChain</filter-name>
    <filter-class>org.springframework.web.filter.DelegatingFilterProxy</filter-class>
</filter>
```

```
    <filter-mapping>
        <filter-name>springSecurityFilterChain</filter-name>
        <url-pattern>/*</url-pattern>
    </filter-mapping>

    <filter>
        <filter-name>HttpMethodFilter</filter-name>
        <filter-class>org.springframework.web.filter.HiddenHttpMethodFilter</filter-class>
    </filter>
    <filter-mapping>
        <filter-name>CharacterEncodingFilter</filter-name>
        <url-pattern>/*</url-pattern>
    </filter-mapping>

    <filter-mapping>
        <filter-name>HttpMethodFilter</filter-name>
        <url-pattern>/*</url-pattern>
    </filter-mapping>

    <!-- Creates the Spring Container shared by all Servlets and Filters -->
    <listener>
        <listener-class>org.springframework.web.context.ContextLoaderListener
        </listener-class>
    </listener>

    <!-- Handles Spring requests -->
    <servlet>
        <servlet-name>spring-mvc</servlet-name>
        <servlet-class>org.springframework.web.servlet.DispatcherServlet</servlet-class>
         <init-param>
            <param-name>contextConfigLocation</param-name>
            <param-value>WEB-INF/spring/applicationContext-web.xml</param-value>
         </init-param>
        <load-on-startup>1</load-on-startup>
    </servlet>

    <servlet-mapping>
        <servlet-name>spring-mvc</servlet-name>
        <url-pattern>/</url-pattern>
    </servlet-mapping>
</web-app>
```

As mentioned earlier, with web-based Spring applications, you ultimately end up with multiple application contexts containing all of your Spring beans. There's a single root application context and potentially many child application contexts.

ContextLoaderListener implements the javax.servlet.ServletContextListener interface. Listeners that implement the ServletContextListener interface receive notifications from the application container whenever the servlet context is initialized or destroyed. It's a convenience mechanism to simplify your application configuration and ease system maintenance. Spring's ContextLoaderListener fires upon receiving such a notification when the servlet context is created during application startup. It expects to find a contextConfigLocation parameter defined in the servlet context, and then uses this parameter to retrieve the bean definitions and instantiates them. The beans outlined by the contextConfigLocation compose what is commonly referred to as the *root application context.*

Servlet Definition

The web.xml file is also where you configure any implementations of the Servlet interface that your application requires. Servlets are configured, along with any initialization parameters the servlet class expects, and then associated with the URL pattern to which you want the servlet to be applied.

For a Spring application, you would take advantage of the framework's DispatcherServlet class. DispatcherServlet is a flexible implementation of the Servlet interface that serves as a central routing mechanism for HTTP requests. With the help of adapter classes offered by Spring, you can specify how each instance of DispatcherServlet handles everything from view resolution to exception handling in a nice, pluggable way.

Each of these instances of DispatcherServlet has its own namespace, commonly referred to as a *child application context.* That means that each DispatcherServlet has its own ApplicationContext, but they all share the root application context. In short, this means that Spring beans defined in the ApplicationContext of a DispatcherServlet may reference the beans from your root ApplicationContext but not vice versa. It also means that separate DispatcherServlet instances may not share their bean definitions.

■ **Note** The ApplicationContext used by each DispatcherServlet is technically an implementation of Spring's WebApplicationContext interface. The WebApplicationContext adds a getServletContext method to the generic ApplicationContext interface. It also defines a well-known application attribute name that the root context must be bound to in the bootstrap process.

Let's take another look at our application's DispatcherServlet definition. Just as with our datasources, we give each configured DispatcherServlet a unique name, because we expect to end up with several.

```
<!-- Handles Spring requests -->
<servlet>
    <servlet-name>spring-mvc</servlet-name>
    <servlet-class>org.springframework.web.servlet.DispatcherServlet</servlet-class>
    <init-param>
        <param-name>contextConfigLocation</param-name>
        <param-value>WEB-INF/spring/applicationContext-web.xml</param-value>
    </init-param>
    <load-on-startup>1</load-on-startup>
</servlet>
```

The servlet is defined with an init-param named contextConfigLocation, which provides the servlet with all the information it needs to acquire and instantiate its Spring bean configuration. And beans in applicationContext-web.xml may safely reference beans the ApplicationContext defined in applicationContext-core.xml and its subsequent imports.

However, there's one large exception to this ApplicationContext hierarchy: implementations of the BeanFactoryPostProcessor interface and its sibling BeanPostProcessor just apply to the BeanFactory that defines them. The PropertyPlaceholderConfigurer class described earlier in this chapter is one such example. This means that you need to define a property placeholder once for each DispatcherServlet in addition to the one already defined in the applicationContext-core.xml root application context.

Finally, we instruct our application container to map any requests that start with / to this dispatcher:

```
<servlet-mapping>
    <servlet-name>spring-mvc</servlet-name>
    <url-pattern>/</url-pattern>
</servlet-mapping>
```

With that configuration in place, a fictitious request to /foo would be mapped to our application's DispatcherServlet, which would in turn route the request to a proper Spring MVC controller.

Spring MVC

Bootstrapping Spring MVC is incredibly simple. The following are the contents of src/main/webapp/WEB-INF/spring/applicationContext-web.xml, which is the configuration file behind our application's DispatcherServlet.

```xml
<?xml version="1.0" encoding="UTF-8" standalone="no"?>
<beans xmlns="http://www.springframework.org/schema/beans"
       xmlns:aop="http://www.springframework.org/schema/aop"
       xmlns:context="http://www.springframework.org/schema/context"
       xmlns:jee="http://www.springframework.org/schema/jee"
       xmlns:tx="http://www.springframework.org/schema/tx"
       xmlns:xsi="http://www.w3.org/2001/XMLSchema-instance"
       xmlns:repository="http://www.springframework.org/schema/data/repository"
       xmlns:mvc="http://www.springframework.org/schema/mvc"
       xsi:schemaLocation="http://www.springframework.org/schema/jee
       http://www.springframework.org/schema/jee/spring-jee-4.1.xsd
       http://www.springframework.org/schema/aop
       http://www.springframework.org/schema/aop/spring-aop-4.1.xsd
       http://www.springframework.org/schema/data/repository
       http://www.springframework.org/schema/data/repository/spring-repository-1.6.xsd
       http://www.springframework.org/schema/beans
       http://www.springframework.org/schema/beans/spring-beans-4.1.xsd
       http://www.springframework.org/schema/tx
       http://www.springframework.org/schema/tx/spring-tx-4.1.xsd
       http://www.springframework.org/schema/context http://www.springframework.org/schema/
       context/spring-context-4.1.xsd ttp://www.springframework.org/schema/mvc
       http://www.springframework.org/schema/mvc/spring-mvc.xsd">

    <context:spring-configured/>

    <context:component-scan base-package="com.apress.springpersistence">
        <context:exclude-filter expression="org.springframework.stereotype.Controller"
        type="annotation"/>
    </context:component-scan>

    <bean id="jsonView" class="org.springframework.web.servlet.view.json.
    MappingJackson2JsonView"/>

</beans>
```

We're using Spring's component scanning again in this WebApplicationContext. This time around, we're specifying an include-filter to restrict the beans we instantiate to only those POJOs annotated with the @Controller stereotype annotation.

Next, we employ the mvc-namespace declaration to turn on support for mapping requests to Spring MVC @Controller methods.

```
<mvc:annotation-driven/>
```

This convenience configuration syntax also registers default Spring formatters and Spring validators for use across all controllers. This allows us to write controller code like the following:

```java
package com.apress.springpersistence.audiomanager.web;

import com.apress.springpersistence.audiomanager.core.repository.AudioObjectRepository;
import com.apress.springpersistence.audiomanager.core.domain.AudioObject;
import org.springframework.beans.factory.annotation.Autowired;
import org.springframework.data.domain.Page;
import org.springframework.data.domain.PageRequest;
import org.springframework.data.domain.Pageable;
import org.springframework.transaction.annotation.Transactional;
import org.springframework.web.bind.annotation.RequestMapping;
import org.springframework.web.bind.annotation.RequestParam;
import org.springframework.web.bind.annotation.ResponseBody;
import org.springframework.web.bind.annotation.RestController;

/**
 * Created by pfisher on 9/27/14.
 */
@RestController
public class AudioController {

    private AudioObjectRepository audioObjectRepository;

    public AudioObjectRepository getAudioObjectRepository() {
        return audioObjectRepository;
    }

    @Autowired
    public void setAudioObjectRepository(AudioObjectRepository audioObjectRepository) {
        this.audioObjectRepository = audioObjectRepository;
    }

    @RequestMapping("/audio")
    @ResponseBody
    @Transactional(readOnly = true)
    public Page<AudioObject> findAllAudio(@RequestParam("page") Integer page) {
        Pageable pageable = new PageRequest(page, 10);
        return this.audioObjectRepository.findAll(pageable);

    }

}
```

This abridged code is annotated as a controller. It's also mapped to /audio via the Spring MVC @RequestMapping annotation. The @RequestParam annotation is used to capture a query parameter specified within an HTTP request, and then convert it to the appropriate type (in this case, an Integer) so that it can be passed in as a method parameter. That's a lot to digest in a short period of time, but suffice it to say, Spring's MVC annotations greatly reduce the amount of code required to build out a full-fledged enterprise web application.

Summary

In this chapter, you got a sense for what is involved in setting up a web application using core Spring, Maven, a database, and Spring MVC.

Maven is a great tool that development teams can use to simplify day-to-day development. You can manage your dependencies, ensuring repeatable build processes, and provide a consistent interface for developers on your team to use for interacting with your project.

You also learned about some of Spring's features, including component scanning, BeanFactoryPostProcessors like the PropertPlaceholderConfigurer, Spring's namespace support, and more advanced XML configuration management with import declarations. Component scanning is likely the most important of these features since it allows Spring to locate classes within a specified package structure so that it can manage these components and resolve dependencies appropriately.

The component-scanning feature allows developers to use annotations as hints for Spring. It simplifies the work required to wire dependencies together and even reduces the amount of XML configuration required. For instance, the @Repository annotation should be used to indicate those classes that compose the DAO layer, the @Service annotation can be used to designate those classes that are part of an application's service facade, and the @Controller annotation denotes the presence of a POJO that should be used for Spring MVC interactions. These annotations simplify the definition of the respective tiers, imbuing layer classes with metadata that helps describe their purpose.

You also saw what's required to integrate a database into a Spring application using the Apache commons-dbcp library for connection pools or via JNDI if you want to use the datasource offerings from your application container.

In the next chapters, we'll build out our domain model and integrate Hibernate into our audio manager application, as well as investigate leveraging Java-based configuration.

CHAPTER 4

■ ■ ■

Persistence with Hibernate

Much like Spring, Hibernate changed the software development landscape when it first appeared on the scene. The timing was ideal. Developers were frustrated by the complexity of J2EE and the overhead associated with using EJB for persistence in particular. Hibernate solves the persistence problem through simplicity and clean, thoughtful design.

Also like Spring, Hibernate relies heavily on POJOs. Other ORM frameworks force developers to muddy their domain model with restrictive and rigid requirements, such as alternate and parent classes, as well as Data Transfer Objects (DTOs). Hibernate enables persistence with little reliance or coupling to Hibernate itself. Spring helps to decouple Hibernate further through several classes of its own, which serve to simplify and standardize integration and persistence operations. Additionally, Spring provides a framework-agnostic solution for implementing transactional behavior in a standardized, declarative fashion, without requiring Hibernate-specific code.

The Spring Data subproject offers additional capabilities beyond what is provided by the core Spring framework. Spring Data provides an abstraction that further decouples your application's persistence tier, offering a generalized API that integrates with relational databases and NoSQL datastores, such as MongoDB, Redis, and SOLR. Spring Data also significantly streamlines the creation of your application's repository implementation, providing useful abstractions for dynamically generating queries, implicit auditing features, and hypermedia-driven RESTful APIs.

Looking back, it is easy to see how Spring and Hibernate were instrumental to each other's success. With philosophies that stressed lightweight methodologies, simplicity, and code cleanliness, the Hibernate/ Spring duo ushered in a new age for enterprise Java applications and persistence. This mutual success had a dramatic impact on the Java community; it was the catalyst to numerous changes that embraced a lighter-weight approach to application development.

There is often a great deal of confusion about the various persistence options in the Java ecosystem. What's the difference between EJB 3, JPA, JDO, and Hibernate anyway? We'll attempt to demystify these things in this chapter by going over a bit of history and defining some terms. With that out of the way, we'll demonstrate how to integrate Hibernate into a Spring application.

The Evolution of Database Persistence in Java

JDBC was included by Sun Microsystems as part of JDK 1.1 in 1997. JDBC is a low-level API that is oriented toward relational databases. It provides methods for querying and updating a database. JDBC provides a great set of tools, but all of the heavy lifting is left entirely to the developer, who must write SQL, map query results to domain objects, manage connections and transactions, and so on. Most other persistence frameworks are built as abstractions on top of JDBC to ease this developer burden.

Beginning in 2000, version 3.0 of the JDBC specification was managed as a part of the Java Community Process (JCP). The JCP was created in 1998 as a mechanism for interested parties to participate in shaping the future directions of the Java platform. The JCP revolves around Java Specification Requests (JSRs),

© Paul Fisher and Brian D. Murphy 2016
P. Fisher and B.D. Murphy, *Spring Persistence with Hibernate*, DOI 10.1007/978-1-4842-0268-5_4

which are formal documents outlining proposed additions or changes to the Java platform. Each JSR has one or more individuals playing the role of specification lead and a team of members referred to as the expert group, who collaborate to hammer out the specification. A final JSR also includes a reference implementation.

This distinction between a *specification* and an *implementation* is one of the primary sources of confusion among developers when discussing the various persistence options available. For example, JPA is a *specification*, and Hibernate is just one of many projects that provide an *implementation* of the JPA specification. Other implementations of the JPA specification include OpenJPA, DataNucleus, and the reference implementation, EclipseLink. But we're getting ahead of ourselves. Let's walk through the origins of some of these specifications and implementations.

EJB, JDO, and JPA

In the late 1990s and early 2000s, the leading technology for developing large-scale applications in Java was EJB. Originally conceived by IBM in 1997, the EJB 1.0 and 1.1 specifications were adopted by Sun in 1999. From there, EJB was enhanced through the JCP. JSR 19 served as the incubator for EJB 2.0, which was finalized in 2001. The EJB 2.0 specification became a major component in Sun's Java 2 Platform, Enterprise Edition (a.k.a J2EE) reference implementation.

There's no question that the problems that EJB set out to solve, including enabling transactional integrity over distributed applications, remote procedure calls (RPC), and ORM, are complex, but EJB quickly earned a reputation for being more trouble than it was worth. The EJB 1.0, 1.1, and 2.0 specifications were marred by the complexities of checked exceptions, required interfaces, and the heavy use of abstract classes. Most applications just didn't require the heft associated with EJB 1 and 2. Against that backdrop, there was a huge opportunity for competition and innovation.

The first official attempt to create a lightweight abstraction layer on top of JDBC by the JCP was JSR 12: Java Data Objects (JDO). The expert group behind JDO set out in 1999 to define a standard way to store Java objects persistently in transactional datastores. In addition, it defined a means for translating data from a relational database into Java objects and a standard way to define the transactional semantics associated with those objects. By the time the specification was finalized in 2002, JDO had evolved into a POJO-based API that was datastore-agnostic. This meant that you could use JDO with many different datastores, ranging from a relational database management system (RDBMS) to a file system, or even with an object-oriented database (OODB). Interestingly, the major application server vendors did not embrace JDO 1.0, so it never took off.

Between JDO and EJB, there were now two competing standards for managing persistence, neither of which was able to break through and win over developers. That left the door open for commercial players and open source frameworks. Hibernate is usually the ORM framework that people think of as replacing EJB 2.0, but another major player actually came first.

An ORM by the name of TopLink was originally developed by The Object People for the Smalltalk programming language. It was ported to Java and added to the company's product line by 1998. TopLink was eventually acquired by Oracle in 2002. TopLink was an impressive framework, and its features played a major role in shaping the persistence specifications that have since emerged in the Java world. As a fringe commercial project, TopLink never saw the level of adoption enjoyed by EJB, which was heavily backed by the application server vendors like IBM and BEA; nor was it able to really compete with the lightweight open source frameworks that emerged, such as Hibernate.

Gavin King set out to build Hibernate in 2001 to provide an alternative to suffering through the well-known problems associated with EJB 2 entity beans. He felt that he was spending more time thinking about persistence than the business problems of his clients. Hibernate was intended to enhance productivity and enable developers to focus more on object modeling, and to simplify the implementation of persistence logic. Hibernate 1.0 was released in 2002, Hibernate 2.0 was released in 2003, and Hibernate 3.0 was released in 2005. Throughout that entire period, Hibernate gained a huge amount of momentum as a free, POJO-based ORM that was well documented and very approachable for developers. Hibernate was able to deliver a means to develop enterprise applications that was practical, simple, elegant, and open source.

Throughout the first five years of Hibernate's existence, it did not adhere to any specification and it wasn't a part of any standards process. Hibernate was just an open source project that you could use to solve real problems and get things done. During this time, many key players—including Gavin King himself—came together to begin working on JSR 220: Enterprise JavaBeans 3.0. Their mission was to create a new standard that remedied the pain points associated with EJBs from a developer's point of view. As the expert group worked through the EJB 3.0 specification, it was determined that the persistence component for interacting with RDBMSs should be broken off into its own API. The Java Persistence API (JPA) was born, building on many of the core concepts that had already been implemented and proven in the field by ORMs like TopLink and Hibernate. As a part of the JSR 220 expert group, Oracle provided the reference implementation of JPA 1.0 with its TopLink product. JSR 220 was finalized in 2006, and EJB 3 played a central role in Sun's definition of Java Enterprise Edition 5, or JEE 5.

■ **Note**   Please pay attention to the change in notation from J2EE to JEE. J2EE is now a legacy designation for the Enterprise Edition of Java. It's time to fix your résumé!

This evolution played out perfectly for JPA. JPA 1.0 was a huge milestone for persistence in Java. However, many features that were essential for developers already using tools like Hibernate didn't make the cut due to time constraints. JPA 2.0 added many important features, including the Criteria API, cache APIs, and enhancements to the Java Persistence Query Language (JPQL), JPA's object-oriented query language. The JPA 2.0 standard was finalized in December 2009 as a new, stand-alone JSR that was targeted for inclusion in the Java EE 6 specification. Oracle donated the source code and development resources for TopLink to Sun in order to create the EclipseLink project. EclipseLink went on to become the reference implementation for JPA 2.0. Hibernate 3.5 was released in the spring of 2010 with full support for JSR 317: JPA 2.0.

JPA 2.1 offers significant improvements to the standard, such as support for *entity graphs*, which allows the details of how object attributes and subgraphs should be fetched to be defined declaratively (as opposed to explicitly defining fetch requirements as part of a specific query). JPA 2.1 also brings improvements to the Criteria API and support for stored procedures. Hibernate 4.3 was the first version of Hibernate to support JPA 2.1. Hibernate 5 also supports this version of the standard and includes further improvements as well.

That's a long and sordid history, but things have worked out quite nicely. JPA now encompasses most of the functionality that you need for developing large-scale enterprise Java applications.

HOW ABOUT JDO?

Persistence standards in Java aren't quite as clear as one might like. You see, JDO is still very much alive and well. JSR 243 ushered in JDO 2.0 in 2006 and has seen several minor revisions since. In many ways, JDO is a superset of JPA. As a result, JDO implementers like DataNucleus have been able to incorporate both the JDO specification and the JPA specification into their products. For a variety of reasons, JDO isn't implemented by Hibernate, and it isn't incorporated into the EJB 3 specification at all. Nevertheless, JDO has been enjoying bit of a resurgence in recent years.

Because JDO is datastore-agnostic, while JPA is wholly about relational datastores, there are many interesting use cases that aren't suitable for JPA but hit a sweet spot for JDO. For instance, JDO is a key ingredient for developing Java applications on the Google App Engine (GAE). GAE is a "platform as a service" (PaaS), which is built on top of Google's BigTable custom datastore rather than an RDBMS.

So why not just use JDO and forgo the creation of JPA in the first place? The reasons for competing specifications are numerous—some technical, some ideological, and some political. The largest companies in the industry heavily influence the JCP, and they obviously sometimes have competing motivations.

How Hibernate Fits In

Now that we've talked about the standards, let's look at where Hibernate fits in and dispel a few common misconceptions.

First of all, Hibernate is not EJB and vice versa. EJB is a specification to provide a distributed, container-managed, server-side component architecture. EJB encapsulates several distinct specifications to facilitate many things, including distributed transaction management, concurrency control, messaging, web services, and security—just to name a few. The EJB specification assumes persistence handling can be delegated to a JPA provider.

Secondly, Hibernate is not JPA. Rather, Hibernate is one of many frameworks that provide a standards-compliant implementation of JPA. The first release of Hibernate to support JPA 1.0 was Hibernate 3.2, which became generally available in the fall of 2006.

Often, there are specialized features provided by frameworks like Hibernate that fall outside the JPA specification. As such, Hibernate can be thought of as a superset of JPA. On one end of the spectrum, Hibernate's architecture allows you to use Hibernate Core without using any parts of the JPA specification at all. On the polar opposite end of the spectrum, you can strictly use only the pieces of Hibernate that adhere to the JPA specification. Strict adherence to the JPA specification ensures true frictionless portability to other JPA implementations, like Apache's OpenJPA project.

When using Hibernate, we recommend that developers stick to the JPA specification as closely as possible—but don't drive yourself crazy. Because open source projects tend to evolve at a much more rapid pace than the JCP, frameworks like Hibernate offer solutions to problems not addressed by the standards process. If these custom offerings ease developer pain, please, please be pragmatic and take advantage of them! This is part of the beauty of the standards process—implementers of the various specifications are free to innovate, and the best, most successful ideas are likely to be incorporated into future revisions of the specification.

The JPA specification defines a set of annotations that can be applied to domain classes in order to map objects to database tables and member variables to columns. JPA also features a SQL-like language called JPQL, which can query the database with an object-oriented flavor. To access your database-mapped domain model, or to execute JPQL queries, you use javax.persistence.EntityManager.

Prior to JPA, Hibernate applications revolved around using Hibernate's SessionFactory and Session interfaces. Simply speaking, Hibernate's SessionFactory is aware of global configuration details, while the Session scope is limited to the current transaction. The JPA EntityManager serves as a cross between Hibernate's SessionFactory and Session; therefore, it is aware of both your database connection configuration and the transaction context. In this chapter, you'll learn a bit about JPQL and EntityManager and how they interact with Spring. Mostly, you'll learn how to go about setting up an application to use Hibernate's implementation of the JPA 2.1 specification.

JPA Interface Hierarchy

Figure 4-1 outlines the four key interfaces in any JPA application. The EntityManagerFactory represents the configuration for a database in your application. You would typically define one EntityManagerFactory per datastore. The EntityManagerFactory is used to create multiple EntityManager instances.

Figure 4-1. *JPA interfaces*

Each EntityManager instance is analogous to a database connection. In a multithreaded web application, each thread will have its own EntityManager.

■ **Note** By default, all Spring objects are singletons. EntityManager is no different, but it is still thread-safe and knows about transactional boundaries. Spring passes in a shared proxy EntityManager, which delegates to a thread-bound instance of the EntityManager that knows all about the context of the request (including transaction boundaries).

Each EntityManager has a single EntityTransaction, which is required for persisting changes to the underlying database. Finally, the EntityManager serves as a factory for generating Query classes. Classes that implement the Query interface are needed for executing queries against the database.

The EntityManagerFactory is relevant only when starting up an application, and we'll show you how that is configured in a Spring application. Querying will be covered in more depth in Chapter 6, and transaction management will be discussed in Chapter 7. As you'll see in this chapter, the EntityManager interface is the interface that you tend to interact with the most.

■ **Note** Since JPA is intended to be used in both heavyweight and lightweight containers, there are many configuration options. For example, you can use an EJB container to configure JPA, and then expose the container's EntityManager for Spring to access via JNDI. Alternatively, you can configure JPA directly within Spring using one of the many existing JPA implementations. One significant difference is the need (or lack thereof) of *load-time weaving*, which is the type of bytecode manipulation required for AOP. Load-time weaving is needed for creating transactionally aware JPA EntityManager and Entity objects that can perform lazy-loading. EJB servers have their own load-time weaving mechanism, and so does Spring. A single EntityManager can handle this type of functionality only through the support of the level of indirection that a proxy can provide. The Hibernate JPA implementation is one of the frameworks that doesn't require load-time weaving, so it allows you to get up and running in a JPA environment as quickly as possible.

The Audio Manager Domain Model and DAO Structure

Now it's time to get back to building our art gallery application. The core thing that we must represent in an audio manager application is an entity for persisting audio and media. In Figure 4-2, you'll see a MediaObject class that represents individual audio or media files. Our application allows users to add Comment and Review entities to these MediaObjects. Note that the MediaObject class extends the CreativeWork class, and that CreateWork extends the Thing class. This class hierarchy allows you to cleanly separate media details, such as raw audio data, bit rate, and sampling details from attribution details, such as an audio element's author and copyright information. We'll explore how this polymorphic hierarchy is implemented later, but the ability to define rich class hierarchies and define how they are mapped to database tables is a very powerful feature of Hibernate that we will leverage throughout this book.

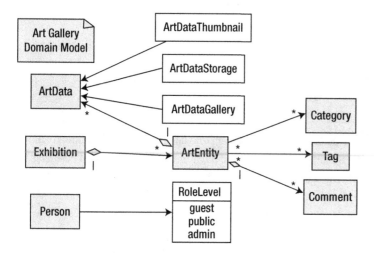

Figure 4-2. *The AudioManager domain model*

We also define a Person type to store information about all users of the application, as well as people associated with the various media elements managed by the application (e.g., the creator of a particular song or podcast). These Person entities are associated with User objects, the latter of which is responsible for storing login details such as username and password.

JPA allows you to specify how a Java class is mapped to the database via annotations. The most important annotation is the @Entity annotation.

An @Entity-Annotated POJO

Adding a JPA @Entity annotation to a POJO makes it a persistable object! Well not quite—you still need to add an @Id somewhere, and ideally, a @Version field, but it's just that simple.

```
package com.apress.springpersistence.audiomanager.core.domain;

import com.apress.springpersistence.audiomanager.core.domain.components.PersonName;
import org.hibernate.validator.constraints.Email;

import javax.persistence.*;
import java.util.Optional;

@Entity
@PrimaryKeyJoinColumn(name="THING_URL")
@Inheritance(strategy=InheritanceType.JOINED)
public class Person extends Thing {
```

```
    @Embedded
    private PersonName personName;

    @Email
    private String email;
    private String gender;
    private String telephone;

    @Transient
    public Optional<String> getGivenName() {
        return Optional.ofNullable(this.personName.getFirstName());
    }

    @Transient
    public Optional<String> getAdditionalName() {
        return Optional.ofNullable(this.personName.getLastName());
    }

    ... getters and setters omitted
}
```

As mentioned earlier, our Person class extends Thing. Notice that we define an @Inheritance annotation, specifying a strategy of InheritanceType.JOINED. This tells Hibernate that we want our class hierarchy to be defined as separate tables in the database that are associated together via a join. For instance, this would mean that querying for a Person entity would actually join both the Person and Thing table from the database. It is also possible to define an entire class hierarchy using a single database table. We will explore these, and other, polymorphic strategies later in this book.

Let's now take a look at the Thing class, which our Person class extends:

```
package com.apress.springpersistence.audiomanager.core.domain;

import org.springframework.data.jpa.domain.AbstractPersistable;

import javax.persistence.*;
import java.net.URL;

@Entity
@Inheritance(strategy= InheritanceType.JOINED)
public class Thing extends AbstractPersistable<Long> {

    @Id
    @GeneratedValue(strategy = GenerationType.AUTO)
    private Long id;

    private URL url;
    private URL additionalType;
    private String alternateName;
    @Column(length = 255)
    private String description;
```

```
    @org.hibernate.validator.constraints.URL
    private URL image;

    @Column(length=255)
    private String name;
//    private Action potentialAction;
    private URL sameAs;

    @Version
    private Integer version;

    public URL getAdditionalType() {
        return additionalType;
    }

    public void setAdditionalType(URL additionalType) {
        this.additionalType = additionalType;
    }

    public String getAlternateName() {
        return alternateName;
    }

    public void setAlternateName(String alternateName) {
        this.alternateName = alternateName;
    }

    public String getDescription() {
        return description;
    }

    public void setDescription(String description) {
        this.description = description;
    }

    public URL getImage() {
        return image;
    }

    public void setImage(URL image) {
        this.image = image;
    }

    public String getName() {
        return name;
    }

    public void setName(String name) {
        this.name = name;
    }
```

```
    public URL getSameAs() {
        return sameAs;
    }

    public void setSameAs(URL sameAs) {
        this.sameAs = sameAs;
    }

    public URL getUrl() {
        return url;
    }

    public void setUrl(URL url) {
        this.url = url;
    }

    public Integer getVersion() {
        return version;
    }

    public void setVersion(Integer version) {
        this.version = version;
    }

    public Long getId() {
        return id;
    }

    public void setId(Long id) {
        this.id = id;
    }
}
```

You'll notice that the Thing class extends a class called AbstractPersistable, which is one of the classes provided by Spring Data that defines useful base constructs. For example, this class includes default equals and hashCode implementations that come in very handy. Spring Data also includes a different base class that offers an implicit auditing capability (for tracking who and when someone created or modified a particular entity).

It's important to note that the AbstractPersistable base class implements Serializable (via the Persistable interface AbstractPersistable implements). Making an entity serializable isn't strictly necessary as far as the JPA specification is concerned. However, it is needed if you're going to use caching or EJB remoting, both of which require objects to be Serializable. Caching is a key component in achieving optimal performance in any JPA application, as you'll learn in Chapter 9, so implementing the Serializable interface is a good habit to adopt.

■ **Note** We've included all of the requisite import statements in the code listings here to help you see where the various annotations are coming from. Annotations are great for eliminating XML, but as the number of annotations on a given class or method grows, they can become a bit hard to read at times. Anything in the javax.persistence package is explicitly provided by JPA.

Unless told otherwise, the JPA implementation employs convention over configuration and maps this bean to a `Person` table. The `@GeneratedValue` JPA annotation tells Hibernate to use an autogenerated `id` column. Hibernate chooses the best ID-generation strategy for the specific database that you're using. Hibernate is also smart enough to determine the right data type for each database column, based on the Java primitive type or enumeration used for each member variable. You can customize these field mappings further through the use of the `@Basic`, `@Enumerated`, `@Temporal`, and `@Lob` annotations. Every member of the entity is assumed to be persistent unless it is static or annotated as `@Transient`. We'll talk more about the convention over configuration concept and Hibernate annotations in Chapter 5.

That's all you need to do from the POJO side, but an `@Entity`-annotated POJO doesn't do anything on its own. At the very least, you need to provide code for basic CRUD operations. For now, we're going to embrace the DAO pattern. We'll explore coding in a more domain-centric style with the Active Record pattern later in this book.

Simplified DAO Pattern with Generics

Let's create a DAO that saves and finds a `Person` entity. We're going to leverage generics so that we can abstract away the boilerplate CRUD operations that would otherwise be repeated over and over again by each DAO in our application.

Please keep in mind that setting up these boilerplate CRUD operations is simplified by using Spring Data's abstractions. We looked at some of these details in Chapters 1 and 2, but we'll examine the implementation more closely here.

In the pseudo-UML shown in Figure 4-3, notice that our `Person` domain object implements an interface called `DomainObject`. That `DomainObject` interface is an empty interface that is used by our `GenericDao` interface as well as our `GenericDaoJpa` concrete class to bind our domain objects in a generic way. This structure enables us to push common methods into the `GenericDaoJpa` class, which in turn, allows us to keep our Hibernate DAOs succinct.

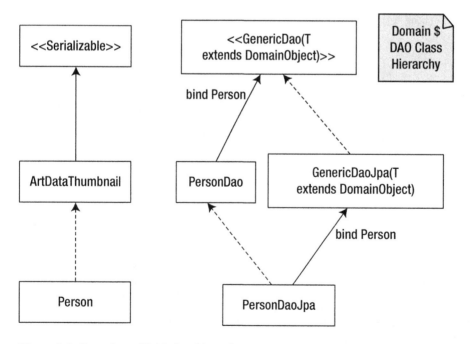

Figure 4-3. *Domain and DAO class hierarchy*

In the diagram shown in Figure 4-3, solid lines represent inheritance. Interface inheritance is depicted with dotted lines. The key usages of Java generics are highlighted by the "bind Person" annotations. Generics in Java allow a type or method to operate on objects of various types while providing compile-time type safety.

Let's see how this plays out in actual code. Spring Data offers a few key abstractions for defining DAO classes. The most basic of these is the Repository interface, but let's take a look at the CrudRepository interface, which provides several useful generic methods:

```
public interface CrudRepository<T, ID extends Serializable> extends Repository<T, ID> {
    <S extends T> S save(S var1);

    <S extends T> Iterable<S> save(Iterable<S> var1);

    T findOne(ID var1);

    boolean exists(ID var1);

    Iterable<T> findAll();

    Iterable<T> findAll(Iterable<ID> var1);

    long count();

    void delete(ID var1);

    void delete(T var1);

    void delete(Iterable<? extends T> var1);

    void deleteAll();
}
```

Each generic type variable is represented as T. As you can see, Spring Data has provided several key methods in this interface that are essential when managing and querying persistent objects. The delete methods will remove a given entity or a collection of entities from the database. The save methods allow us to insert or update a single or multiple entities. Finally, there is a count method, as well as integral methods for querying by ID or simply iterating through all the instances of a particular entity.

An even more useful Spring Data abstraction is the PagingAndSortingRepository, which extends the CrudRepository by adding sort and pagination features, which are usually critical for most production applications.

Let's now take a look at how we can leverage these abstractions in our application. We'll start by defining our UserRepository class:

```
package com.apress.springpersistence.audiomanager.core.repository;

import com.apress.springpersistence.audiomanager.core.domain.User;
import org.springframework.data.domain.Pageable;
import org.springframework.data.domain.Slice;
import org.springframework.data.repository.CrudRepository;
import org.springframework.data.repository.query.Param;
import org.springframework.data.rest.core.annotation.RepositoryRestResource;
```

```
@Repository
public interface UserRepository extends CrudRepository<User, String> {

    public User findByUsernameAndPasswordHash(@Param("username") String username,
    @Param("passwordHash") String passwordHash);

    public Slice<User> findByPersonPersonNameLastNameOrderByPersonPersonNameLastNameAsc
    (@Param("lastName") String lastName, Pageable pageable);

    public Slice<User> findByPersonPersonNameFirstNameOrderByPersonPersonNameFirstNameAsc
    (@Param("firstName") String firstName, Pageable pageable);

    public Slice<User> findByPersonPersonNameFirstNameAndPersonPersonNameLastName
    OrderByPersonPersonNameLastNameAsc(@Param("firstName") String firstName,
    @Param("lastName") String lastName, Pageable pageable);

}
```

Notice that this implementation is actually quite small. In fact, we could have just defined the following interface:

```
@Repository
public interface UserRepository extends CrudRepository<User, String> {

}
```

Even though the preceding UserRepository looks empty, we still inherit all of the core generified methods that we saw in the CrudRepository. For instance, we would now be able to query a User by ID using the following method call:

```
Long userId = 1234L;
User user = userRepository.findOne(userId);
```

As we've discussed, EntityManager is the core mechanism for interacting with JPA. It performs data-access operations in a transaction-aware manner. With it, our UserRepository class can perform basic CRUD tasks: finding single or multiple instances of the class, as well as saving, updating, and deleting an instance.

Another detail to notice is that our Dao classes are annotated with the @Repository annotation. The Spring @Repository annotation has three primary purposes in this example:

- It tells Spring that this class can be imported via classpath scanning.

- It's a marker for Spring to know that this class requires DAO-specific RuntimeException handling.

- We specify the name to be used in the Spring context to represent this class. By specifying that the DAO should be recognized as personDao, via @Repository("personDao"), we can refer to this DAO elsewhere in our Spring configuration simply as personDao, rather than personDaoJpa. This allows us to change the underlying DAO implementation to something else with far less friction.

Using the @Repository annotation allows us to quickly group all DAOs through IDE searching. It also lets a reader know at a glance that this class is a DAO.

Because of our use of generics, the code that remains in the `PersonDaoJpa` implementation is nice and short, and relevant only to the `Person` domain class. Developers are often intimidated by generics, but they can help you avoid doing a lot of rote, repetitive work that adds no value.

The Life Cycle of a JPA Entity

Let's take a closer look at how JPA actually handles our `Person` entity internally. Figure 4-4 highlights the various states that an entity might be in, some of the key methods involved, and a handful of useful annotations for intercepting calls to modify behavior with cross-cutting aspects.

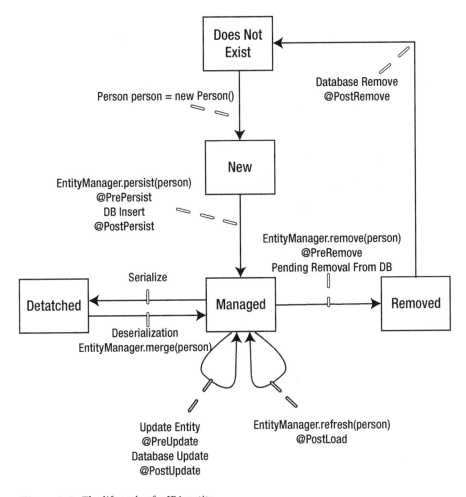

Figure 4-4. *The life cycle of a JPA entity*

There are five key states: Does Not Exist, New, Managed, Removed, and Detached. In addition, there are seven life-cycle callback annotations. The callback annotations, when implemented within your entity class, are referred to as *internal callback methods*. Alternatively, they can be defined outside a given entity class as a listener class. These are referred to as *external callback methods*. You may implement any subset of the callback methods or none at all. You may apply only a specific life-cycle callback to a single method.

You may use multiple callbacks on the same method by applying all of the annotations that apply. You can also use both internal callbacks and external callbacks on a single entity. The external callbacks fire first, and then the internal callbacks are executed. There are a ton of options for taking advantage of these callbacks.

■ **Note** Callback methods should not interact with other entity objects or make calls to `EntityManager` or `Query` methods, to avoid conflicts with the original database operation that is still in progress.

Let's walk through a fictitious life cycle for a person through each of the five key states:

- *Does Not Exist*: We start here.

- *New*: A new person object is instantiated via `Person person = new Person()`. At this stage, the person object is in the New state. It is not associated with an `EntityManager`. and it has no representation in the database. Also, because we're using an autogenerated strategy for our primary key, the object is in memory but has no ID associated with it. Again, this is something to be wary of when managing objects in collections, as an entity has the potential to break the `equals()` and `hashCode()` contract if an object's equality is based off its identifier and this property suddenly changes from null to a real value upon being persisted via Hibernate. We will discuss this issue in more detail in Chapter 5.

- *Managed*: We persist the person entity with a call to `EntityManager.persist()`. If we have a method annotated with `@PrePersist`, that method is executed followed by an insert into the database, optionally followed by the execution of any custom method we've annotated with `@PostPersist`. Now our person entity is in the Managed state. In this state, there are many things that could happen to our person entity. For instance, we could make a call to `EntityManager.refresh()`, which would discard the object in memory and retrieve a fresh copy from the database, optionally taking advantage of the `@PostLoad` callback. Or we could delete the entity via `EntityManager.remove()` resulting in a call to `@PreRemove`.

- *Remove*: Once the record is deleted from the database, the entity is in a Removed state, pending execution of a method annotated with `@PostRemove` before returning to the Does Not Exist state.

- *Detached*: The Detached state comes into play when the object is no longer associated with an `EntityManager` or persistence context. Detached objects are often returned from a persistence tier to the web layer where they can be displayed to the end-user in some form. Changes can be made to a detached object, but these changes won't be persisted to the database until the entity is reassociated with a persistence context.

JPA Configuration

A few pieces of the puzzle remain. Before we have a fully working system, we need to do the following:

- Set up a JPA environment that knows about our `Person` domain object.
- Configure a database connection.
- Manage the system's transactions.
- Inject all of that into the DAO.

We'll first look at the setup from the JPA side, and then handle the Spring side of the configuration.

Bare-Bones JPA Setup

For the typical case, JPA requires you to create a `META-INF/persistence.xml` file. Here is an example of a straightforward configuration:

```xml
<?xml version="1.0" encoding="UTF-8" standalone="no"?>
<persistence xmlns="http://xmlns.jcp.org/xml/ns/persistence"
             xmlns:xsi="http://www.w3.org/2001/XMLSchema-instance" version="2.1"
             xsi:schemaLocation="http://xmlns.jcp.org/xml/ns/persistence
             http://java.sun.com/xml/ns/persistence/persistence_2_1.xsd">
    <persistence-unit name="persistenceUnit"
                      transaction-type="RESOURCE_LOCAL">
        <provider>org.hibernate.jpa.HibernatePersistenceProvider</provider>
        <mapping-file>META-INF/orm.xml</mapping-file>
        <shared-cache-mode>ENABLE_SELECTIVE</shared-cache-mode>

        <properties>
            <property name="hibernate.dialect" value="org.hibernate.dialect.H2Dialect"/>
            <!--
                value='create' to build a new database on each run;
                value='update' to modify an existing database;
                value='create-drop' to create and drop tables on each run;
                value='validate' makes no changes to the database
             -->
            <property name="hibernate.hbm2ddl.auto" value="create"/>
            <property name="hibernate.show_sql" value="true"/>
            <property name="hibernate.cache.use_second_level_cache" value="true"/>
            <property name="hibernate.cache.provider_class"
                      value="net.sf.ehcache.hibernate.SingletonEhCacheProvider"/>
            <property name="hibernate.implicit_naming_strategy"
                      value="org.hibernate.boot.model.naming.
                      ImplicitNamingStrategyJpaCompliantImpl"/>

        </properties>

    </persistence-unit>

</persistence>
```

This creates a persistence unit called `audioManager`. It's recommended that you name your persistence unit in a way that expresses the relationship to a given database so that you may easily incorporate more datastores later without your bean definitions getting too confusing. Typically, we will want all classes annotated with `@Entity` to be added to this persistence unit.

Although configuring JPA via `persistence.xml` is a viable approach, there is a more Spring-centric approach that offers more flexibility and better integration with other Spring-based configuration options. We are going to examine this approach next.

MORE JPA CONFIGURATION OPTIONS

In the `persistence.xml` file, you can optionally configure which classes you want to include for a given unit, but generally, that's necessary only for more complicated scenarios, such as managing multiple databases in a single application. When you do need to map entities to a particular `persistence-unit`, add `<class>` elements to the `persistence.xml` like so:

```xml
<?xml version="1.0" encoding="UTF-8" standalone="no"?>
<persistence xmlns="http://xmlns.jcp.org/xml/ns/persistence"
             xmlns:xsi="http://www.w3.org/2001/XMLSchema-instance" version="2.1"
             xsi:schemaLocation="http://xmlns.jcp.org/xml/ns/persistence
             http://java.sun.com/xml/ns/persistence/persistence_2_1.xsd">
    <persistence-unit name="audioManager"
                      transaction-type="RESOURCE_LOCAL">
        <provider>org.hibernate.jpa.HibernatePersistenceProvider</provider>
        <mapping-file>META-INF/orm.xml</mapping-file>
        <class>com.apress.springpersistence.audiomanager.core.domain.Person</class>

        <shared-cache-mode>ENABLE_SELECTIVE</shared-cache-mode>
        <properties>
            <property name="hibernate.dialect" value="org.hibernate.dialect.H2Dialect"/>

            <property name="hibernate.hbm2ddl.auto" value="update"/>
            <property name="hibernate.show_sql" value="true"/>
            <property name="hibernate.cache.use_second_level_cache" value="true"/>
            <property name="hibernate.cache.provider_class"
                      value="net.sf.ehcache.hibernate.SingletonEhCacheProvider"/>
            <property name="hibernate.implicit_naming_strategy"
                      value="org.hibernate.boot.model.naming.
                      ImplicitNamingStrategyJpaCompliantImpl"/>

        </properties>

    </persistence-unit>

</persistence>
```

There's also the concept of mapping files. Rather than define classes inline, you can declare a mapping file that's referred to in the `persistence.xml` file in a `<mapping-file>` element. That file allows you to declare entity classes, and even override mapping configuration, such as column names and the mechanisms for retrieving IDs. This approach also lets you map classes that don't have any JPA annotations whatsoever.

The `persistence.xml` can also be used to define implementation-specific properties, such as Hibernate properties. Spring's JPA configuration requires you to configure these properties in `persistence.xml` in a `<properties><property>` element. Unfortunately, that means that you won't be able to put your environment-specific configuration details in a Spring property file without getting fancier with your build scripts.

JPA is extremely configurable and feature-rich. For more details on the `persistence.xml` configuration file, see a book devoted to the topic, such as *Pro JPA 2: Mastering the Java Persistence API* by Mike Keith and Merrick Schincariol (Apress, 2009).

Spring Integration

We need a way to create a usable `EntityManager` in the Spring `ApplicationContext`. In typical Spring fashion, there is more than one way to configure JPA. Let's examine a few of the most useful approaches.

The first approach follows a very similar strategy to the one described earlier. We follow the standard JPA conventions and direct Spring to the `persistence.xml` file, which contains most of the JPA-specific configuration:

- A `LocalEntityManagerFactoryBean` uses JPA's standard bootstrapping. `LocalEntityManagerFactoryBean` requires the JPA provider (for example, Hibernate or OpenJPA) to set up everything it needs, including database connections and a provider-specific load-time weaving setup. The bean would look something like this:

```
<bean id="entityManagerFactory"
      class="org.springframework.orm.jpa.LocalEntityManagerFactoryBean">
    <property name="persistenceUnitName" value="audioManager"/>
</bean>
```

If we want to configure this `EntityManagerFactory` via Java configuration, then we can use the following approach instead:

```
@Configuration
@EnableConfigurationProperties
@EnableTransactionManagement
@EnableJpaRepositories(basePackages = {"com.apress.springpersistence.audiomanager.core.
repository"})
@PropertySource("classpath:jpa.properties")
public class JpaConfig {

@Bean
public LocalEntityManagerFactoryBean entityManagerFactory() {
    LocalEntityManagerFactoryBean lef = new LocalEntityManagerFactoryBean();
    lef.setPersistenceUnitName("audioManager");
    lef.setJpaVendorAdapter(jpaVendorAdapter());
    lef.setJpaDialect(jpaDialect());
    return lef;
}

@Bean
public JpaVendorAdapter jpaVendorAdapter() {
    HibernateJpaVendorAdapter hibernateJpaVendorAdapter = new HibernateJpaVendorAdapter();
    hibernateJpaVendorAdapter.setShowSql(jpaConfigurationProperties.isShowSql());
    hibernateJpaVendorAdapter.setGenerateDdl(true);
    hibernateJpaVendorAdapter.setDatabasePlatform(jpaConfigurationProperties.getDialect());

    return hibernateJpaVendorAdapter;
}
```

```
@Bean
public JpaDialect jpaDialect() {
    JpaDialect jpaDialect = new HibernateJpaDialect();
    return jpaDialect;
}

}
```

If you have a Java EE container and you want to use EJB 3, you can use Spring's built-in JNDI lookup capabilities:

```
<jee:jndi-lookup id="entityManagerFactory" jndi-name="persistence/audioManager"/>
```

Using the LocalContainerEntityManagerFactoryBean

The Spring JPA LocalContainerEntityManagerFactoryBean requires a bit more Spring configuration than the other two options. However, it also gives you the most Spring capabilities. Setting up a LocalContainerEntityManagerFactoryBean requires you to configure a datasource and JPA vendor-specific adapters, so that the generic Spring JPA configuration can set up some of the extras required for each vendor. This is the approach that we'll take in this chapter.

We're going to use some of the Java-based Spring configuration that we touched on earlier. We'll also use component scanning to tell Spring to automatically create DAOs found in specific packages.

Let's create a class called JpaConfig. This file will configure the LocalContainerEntityManagerFactoryBean, our datasource, a JPA transaction manager, and annotation-based transactions. The following listing configures all of these important details in a single class file.

```
package com.apress.springpersistence.audiomanager.core.config;

@Configuration
@EnableConfigurationProperties
@EnableTransactionManagement
@EnableJpaRepositories(basePackages = {"com.apress.springpersistence.audiomanager.core.
repository"})
@EntityScan({"com.apress.springpersistence.audiomanager.core.domain"})
@PropertySource("classpath:jpa.properties")
public class JpaConfig {

    @Autowired
    private Environment environment;

    @Autowired
    private DataSourceConfigurationPropertiesBean dataSourceProperties;

    @Autowired
    private JpaConfigurationPropertiesBean jpaConfigurationProperties;

    /**
     * This datasource will only be active when the EmbeddedDb profile is NOT active
     * @return
     */
```

```java
@Profile("!"+ Profiles.EmbeddedDb)
@Bean
public DataSource localDataSource() {
    DataSourceBuilder factory = DataSourceBuilder
            .create(this.getClass().getClassLoader())
            .driverClassName(this.dataSourceProperties.getDriverClassName())
            .url(this.dataSourceProperties.getUrl())
            .username(this.dataSourceProperties.getUsername())
            .password(this.dataSourceProperties.getPassword());
    return factory.build();
}


@Profile(Profiles.EmbeddedDb)
@Bean
public DataSource dataSource() {
    EmbeddedDatabaseBuilder builder = new EmbeddedDatabaseBuilder();
    return builder.setType(EmbeddedDatabaseType.DERBY).build();
}


@Bean
public LocalContainerEntityManagerFactoryBean entityManagerFactory() {
    LocalContainerEntityManagerFactoryBean lef = new
    LocalContainerEntityManagerFactoryBean();
    lef.setDataSource(localDataSource());
    lef.setJpaVendorAdapter(jpaVendorAdapter());
    lef.setJpaDialect(jpaDialect());
    lef.setMappingResources();
    Properties props = new Properties();
    props.put("hibernate.show_sql", jpaConfigurationProperties.isShowSql());
    props.put("hibernate.format_sql", jpaConfigurationProperties.isFormalSql());
//      props.put("hibernate.ejb.naming_strategy", "org.springframework.boot.orm.jpa.
        hibernate.SpringNamingStrategy");
    props.put("hibernate.implicit_naming_strategy", environment.getProperty("spring.jpa.
    hibernate.implicit_naming_strategy"));
    props.put("hibernate.connection.charSet", environment.getProperty("spring.jpa.
    conection.charset"));
    props.put("hibernate.current_session_context_class", jpaConfigurationProperties.
    getCurrentSessionContextClass());
    props.put("hibernate.archive.autodetection", jpaConfigurationProperties.
    getAutodetection());
    props.put("hibernate.transaction.manager_lookup_class", jpaConfigurationProperties.
    getTransactionManagerLookupClass());
    props.put("hibernate.dialect", jpaConfigurationProperties.getDialect());
    props.put("hibernate.hbm2ddl.auto", environment.getProperty("spring.jpa.hbm2ddl.
    auto"));
    lef.setJpaProperties(props);

    lef.afterPropertiesSet();

    return lef;
}
```

```
@Bean
public JpaVendorAdapter jpaVendorAdapter() {
    HibernateJpaVendorAdapter hibernateJpaVendorAdapter = new HibernateJpaVendorAdapter();
    hibernateJpaVendorAdapter.setShowSql(jpaConfigurationProperties.isShowSql());
    hibernateJpaVendorAdapter.setGenerateDdl(true);
    hibernateJpaVendorAdapter.setDatabasePlatform(jpaConfigurationProperties.getDialect());

    return hibernateJpaVendorAdapter;
}

@Bean
public JpaDialect jpaDialect() {
    JpaDialect jpaDialect = new HibernateJpaDialect();
    return jpaDialect;
}

@Bean
public JpaTransactionManager transactionManager() {
    JpaTransactionManager transactionManager = new JpaTransactionManager();

    transactionManager.setEntityManagerFactory(entityManagerFactory().getObject());
    return transactionManager;
}

}
```

Note that we have set up two different datasources: an embedded Derby database and a non-embedded database that uses datasourceProperties that were injected into the JpaConfig configuration class, which allows us to externalize details such as the database URL, username, and password. We then utilize Profiles to tell Spring which datasource we want to use at runtime. If the EmbeddedDb profile is active when our app starts, then we will use the embedded Derby database. Otherwise, we will use our non-embedded database.

We're using LocalContainerEntityManagerFactoryBean, which creates a JPA EntityManager according to JPA's stand-alone bootstrap contract. However, rather than specify JPA configuration details within the persistence.xml file, we have the flexibility to configure a DataSource and transactionManager directly via Spring config. Additionally, we can have Spring discover our entity classes that comprise our application's domain model via the @EntityScan annotation on our JpaConfig class.

The LocalContainerEntityManagerFactoryBean can use a Spring-managed datasource and a few Hibernate-specific properties, such as showSql, generateDdl, and databasePlatform, which are injected via the JpaVendorAdapter bean.

Our Repository classes (annotated with the @Repository annotation) are picked up as a result of the @EnableJpaRepositories at the top of our JpaConfig class, along with the basePackages that we specify as part of this annotation. This annotation provides several configuration options that allow us to customize the way that our Repository layer is implemented and customized. We will examine querying and building a powerful Repository layer in Chapter 6.

Finally, our JpaConfig class also sets up a transactionManager, which defines transactional behavior for our application, and how transactions are defined. In this example, we are using local transactions, which are limited to a single datasource. However, if we wanted to use JTA transactions and have transactions span across multiple datasources or resources, we can easily activate these capabilities simply by adjusting this configuration!

As you've seen, there is a fair amount involved in JPA configuration, but the amount of functionality that is delivered makes it definitely worth the effort!

Querying and DAO Strategies

If the domain model serves as the persistence tier's foundation, then the DAO layer might be considered the engine. As you've learned in previous chapters, the DAO pattern is intended to abstract lower-level persistence functionality, including creating, reading, updating, and deleting entities. But a DAO typically provides more than basic CRUD functionality.

Specialized queries that reflect the core entity-access capability of an application are usually baked into a DAO layer. For example, since our media manager application requires that end users be able to access a series of media files within a particular category, the ability to query and load the relevant MediaObject domain objects by a specified Category should be provided by a DAO class. In other words, you can think of an application's DAO classes as the building blocks utilized by the service layer to provide the necessary persistence-related functionality for the application. We will discuss the service layer in the next chapter, but it is helpful to keep in mind that the service layer typically encapsulates an application's business logic, relying on the DAO layer to get the persistence dirty work done.

One of the reasons that the DAO pattern is considered a best practice is that it helps to abstract the persistence implementation details (and technology) from the DAO interface. This allows application developers to settle on the methods and features of a particular DAO, extracting these specifics into the interface. The DAO interface then becomes the integration hub between the actual persistence implementation and the service layer—the contact for lower-level persistence functionality. This is another area where Spring can help to decouple these components.

In some of the earlier DAO examples in this chapter, we used the @Repository annotation, indicating that we are configuring a class with persistence-related functionality. This annotation is used by Spring's component-scanning facility, which we introduced in Chapter 3. With component scanning, Spring searches a specified package structure to find those classes annotated as components so that they can be managed by Spring and play a role in dependency injection.

Spring defines three core stereotype annotations, each representing a layer within a typical application:

- @Repository is used to delineate those classes that provide *data repository* functionality. In this case, it is our DAO implementation, as it serves the purpose of abstracting all data-access functionality that relates to the Category domain object.

- @Controller is used to delineate controller classes, which are used in the web layer to handle requests.

- @Service defines a service facade. Typically, the service layer wraps the DAO layer, providing a coherent, transactional service that often serves as the business logic for an application. The service layer is often called a *façade*, since it serves as an abstraction over the data-access code, hiding the lower-level implementation details and providing a business-specific API. We will discuss the service layer in more detail in Chapter 8.

These three annotations logically extend from the @Component annotation, which defines any bean intended to be managed by the Spring container. In fact, we could just as easily have used @Component instead of @Repository in our example, but we would lose the intention of our class as a DAO. In other words, we use the @Repository annotation to clue Spring in to the fact that our class is a DAO.

Looking at the JPA Criteria API

In using Hibernate, there are quite a few options available when it comes to querying. Although HQL and JPQL are effective and concise strategies for expressing a query, they both suffer from a few limitations. First, because these query languages are articulated as plain text, they are prone to errors that are unable to be caught or verified by the compiler. Methods containing significant errors in the HQL or JPQL queries will compile perfectly, only to throw exceptions at runtime— or perform in unexpected ways.

HQL and JPQL are also not conducive to expressing dynamic queries, in which the attributes of the query are not fully known until runtime. For instance, if we would like our users to be able to search for images by specifying any number of tags, it would be difficult to represent this sort of query using HQL or JPQL. To accomplish this, we might try dynamically generating a JPQL query string by concatenating the conditions of each tag parameter. Clearly, this is a fragile and awkward solution to this problem.

To address these limitations, Hibernate offers the Criteria API. Until recently, JPA did not include a Criteria API, forcing developers that needed this type of functionality to go outside of the JPA standard. However, with the release of JPA 2.0, a standards-based Criteria API is now available.

Using the JPA 2.0 Criteria API

We've focused more on Hibernate-specific querying, so let's examine the new JPA 2.0 Criteria API. To illustrate the Criteria API, we will define a new DAO method for our MediaObjectDao interface:

```
public List<MediaObject> getMediaByName(String name);
```

This method returns all those MediaObject instances that match the specified title. Obviously, we could express this query using JPQL, however, the Criteria API offers some advantages. One of the primary benefits is that we can leverage compile-time checking to ensure that our query is valid and fits within the constraints of our domain model. Later in this section, we will examine additional Criteria API advantages, such as applying dynamic constraints on our query, including pagination, filtering, and ordering details.

First, let's take a look at our query:

```
public List<MediaObject> getMediaByName(String name) {
    CriteriaBuilder criteriaBuilder = entityManager.getCriteriaBuilder();
    CriteriaQuery<MediaObject> criteriaQuery =
        criteriaBuilder.createQuery(MediaObject.class);
    Root< MediaObject > root = criteriaQuery.from(MediaObject.class);
    Path<String> path = root.<String>get("name");
    criteriaQuery.where(criteriaBuilder.equal(path, name));
    return entityManager.createQuery(criteriaQuery).getResultList();
}
```

If you consider the structure of a JPQL query, you should be able to infer what the preceding method is doing. The first line gets a reference to a CriteriaBuilder, which is a class that is necessary for generating important aspects of the Criteria query, as you will see shortly. The next line uses the CriteriaBuilder reference to create a CriteriaQuery instance. Notice that we pass MediaObject.class as the single parameter to the createQuery method. We are essentially requesting a generically typed CriteriaQuery instance using the MediaObject type. Our intention is to specify that the query return results of type MediaObject. This doesn't necessarily imply that we are querying against a MediaObject instance. In fact, we could specify a type of Long.class to the createQuery method to indicate that our query should return a Long, which is typical when performing projection or aggregate queries.

Now that we have our CriteriaQuery instance, we need to declare what type we intend to query against. We call the from method on our CriteriaQuery instance, specifying a MediaObject parameter. This line of code is similar to a JPQL clause that reads: "from MediaObject". In other words, we are expressing our intention to query against the MediaObject type. A Root instance returns as a result of this method call, which is generically typed to the MediaObject instance. The Root instance can be used as a means for referencing properties on the MediaObject class that we want to use as conditions in our query.

The next line in our method uses the Root instance to access the name field in the MediaObject domain class by calling the get method on the Root instance and specifying the string "title" (which is the appropriate property name in the MediaObject class). This returns a Path instance, which we can use to represent the title property in order to express a condition in our query. To express this condition, we call the where method in the CriteriaQuery instance. Notice that as a parameter to the where method, we have used a criteriaBuilder.equal(path, title) nested method call. We use criteriaBuilder as a factory to construct the equal condition, which returns a Predicate instance. Predicates represent encapsulated logic that return either true or false, and are used as building blocks in the Criteria API to form complex queries. In our case, we have created a Predicate to represent the comparison logic between the Path instance (which represents our MediaObject.name field) and the String title parameter that was passed in to this method.

Now that we've articulated the requirements and conditions for CriteriaQuery, we need to actually execute our query so that we can access the results. This part of the method works in a similar fashion to executing a JPQL query. We invoke createQuery on the EntityManager reference, passing in the CriteriaQuery instance. The createQuery method actually returns a TypedQuery instance that is generically typed to the MediaObject domain class. However, to keep the method streamlined, we call getResultList() on the method chain to directly return a List of MediaObject instances that match our query's conditions.

You're probably thinking that the prior example required quite a bit of work to define a query that might be defined in JPQL as this:

```
public List< MediaObject > getMediaObjectsByName(String name) {
    Query query = this.entityManager.createQuery(
        "select media from MediaObject where media.name = :name "
    );
    query.setParameter("name", name);
    return query.getResultList();
}
```

It's true that the JPQL version is a bit more concise. However, what about our earlier concerns about a lack of compile-time checking on the validity of our query? With the Criteria API approach, we benefit from some assurance that the syntax of our query is verifiable, whereas in JPQL we won't be aware of issues until runtime. However, in our Criteria API example, we are actually short-changing ourselves a bit. Remember that in order to represent the MediaObject.name field as a Path reference, we used the following code:

```
Path<String> path = root.<String>get("name");
```

This line is intuitive, but we are still opening ourselves up to the potential for error, because we could misspell our title field or specify a domain class property that simply doesn't exist. Additionally, when we get into more complex queries, such as those involving associations, we could lose track of the correct field type or plurality.

To address this problem, the JPA 2.0 Criteria API provides a MetaModel, which can be used to describe the metadata related to your domain model. While it is possible to manually define your own MetaModel, in order to mirror the structure of each of your domain classes, the easier bet is to use the Java 1.6 annotation processing feature. Hibernate offers the hibernate-jpamodelgen jar, which can be used to analyze your domain model classes and then automatically generate the source code for the MetaModel. The first step in getting this to work is to add the hibernate-jpamodelgen to your Maven pom.xml file as a dependency:

```
<dependency>
    <groupId>org.hibernate</groupId>
    <artifactId>hibernate-jpamodelgen</artifactId>
    <version>1.0.0.Final</version>
</dependency>
```

Once you've added this dependency, you will be able to have your MetaModel automatically generated and updated whenever your code is compiled. Although it is possible to make this process more implicit, we recommend installing a Maven plugin to provide some level of control and configuration. For example, you will probably want to specify where the MetaModel classes should be located. Copy the following plugin configuration into the <plugins> block of your pom.xml:

```
<plugin>
  <artifactId>maven-compiler-plugin</artifactId>
  <configuration>
    <source>1.6</source>
    <target>1.6</target>
    <compilerArguments>
      <processor>
        org.hibernate.jpamodelgen.JPAMetaModelEntityProcessor
      </processor>
    </compilerArguments>
  </configuration>
</plugin>

<plugin>
  <groupId>org.bsc.maven</groupId>
  <artifactId>maven-processor-plugin</artifactId>
  <executions>
    <execution>
      <id>process</id>
      <goals>
        <goal>process</goal>
      </goals>
      <phase>generate-sources</phase>
      <configuration>
        <!-- source output directory -->
        <outputDirectory>src/main/generated-java</outputDirectory>
      </configuration>
    </execution>
  </executions>
</plugin>

<plugin>
  <groupId>org.codehaus.mojo</groupId>
  <artifactId>build-helper-maven-plugin</artifactId>
  <version>1.3</version>
  <executions>
    <execution>
      <id>add-source</id>
      <phase>generate-sources</phase>
      <goals>
        <goal>add-source</goal>
      </goals>
      <configuration>
```

```
      <sources>
        <source>src/main/generated-java</source>
      </sources>
    </configuration>
  </execution>
  </executions>
</plugin>
```

It may also be necessary to add a <pluginrepositories> block to your pom.xml if you have trouble automatically installing the plugins. You can add the following block to ensure that the necessary plugins can be downloaded:

```
<pluginRepositories>
  <pluginRepository>
    <id>maven-annotation</id>
    <url>
      http://maven-annotation-plugin.googlecode.com/svn/trunk/mavenrepo/
    </url>
  </pluginRepository>
</pluginRepositories>
```

Once you've updated your Maven configuration, you should be able to run mvn compile to trigger the annotation processing for generating the MetaModel. The preceding Maven configuration generates the MetaModel source to src/main/generated-java, but feel free to update the location to suit your own needs.

Once you have generated your MetaModel, you should be able to find these classes in the appropriate location. The MetaModel classes mirror your own domain model classes, except that an underscore is suffixed to the class name. For instance, our MediaObject domain class would have a corresponding MetaModel class in the same package structure but with the name MediaObject_.

Using QueryDSL

While the JPA 2.0 Criteria API offers benefits in terms of type safety, the steps required for expressing a query become a bit convoluted, as mentioned earlier. To help mitigate this problem, a project called QueryDSL has gained significant popularity. Not only does QueryDSL provide a generic and type-safe querying abstraction, it also works across a range of different persistence technologies, including JPA, JDO, MongoDB, and Lucene. Furthermore, QueryDSL also offers a much simpler and more flexible approach for querying. As a result, it was integrated into Spring Data and it has become a very popular tool for querying inHibernate and JPA.

The first step in setting up QueryDSL is to add the necessary dependencies to your Maven configuration (the pom.xml). First, add the QueryDSL dependency:

```
<dependency>
    <groupId>com.mysema.querydsl</groupId>
    <artifactId>querydsl-jpa</artifactId>
    <version>${querydsl.version}</version>
</dependency>
```

You also need to add the appropriate property so that the version value of ${querydsl.version} can be resolved:

```
<querydsl.version>3.7.0</querydsl.version>
```

Similar to the JPA 2.0 Criteria AP, QueryDSL relies on generating query classes to provide a type-safe way for expressing queries. To facilitate this generation, you need to add the following plugin snippet to your maven configuration within the build.plugins block:

```
<plugin>
    <groupId>com.mysema.maven</groupId>
    <artifactId>maven-apt-plugin</artifactId>
    <version>1.0</version>
    <executions>
        <execution>
            <phase>generate-sources</phase>
            <goals>
                <goal>process</goal>
            </goals>
            <configuration>
                <outputDirectory>target/generated-sources</outputDirectory>
                <processor>com.mysema.query.apt.jpa.JPAAnnotationProcessor</processor>
            </configuration>
        </execution>
    </executions>

</plugin>
```

Now, you can run mvn compile. Your QueryDSL query classes will be generated into the target/generated-sources directory.

You will notice that the QueryDSL generated classes all start with a Q prefix, but are contained within the same package structure as your domain entities.

Let's take a look at one of the generated QueryDSL query classes:

```
/**
 * QPerson is a Querydsl query type for Person
 */
@Generated("com.mysema.query.codegen.EntitySerializer")
public class QPerson extends EntityPathBase<Person> {

    private static final long serialVersionUID = -1412701716L;

    private static final PathInits INITS = PathInits.DIRECT2;

    public static final QPerson person = new QPerson("person");

    public final QThing _super = new QThing(this);

    //inherited
    public final SimplePath<java.net.URL> additionalType = _super.additionalType;

    //inherited
    public final StringPath alternateName = _super.alternateName;
```

```java
//inherited
public final DateTimePath<java.util.Date> createdDate = _super.createdDate;

//inherited
public final StringPath description = _super.description;

public final StringPath email = createString("email");

public final com.apress.springpersistence.audiomanager.core.domain.components.
QPersonName fullName;

public final EnumPath<Gender> gender = createEnum("gender", Gender.class);

//inherited
public final NumberPath<Long> id = _super.id;

//inherited
public final DateTimePath<java.util.Date> lastmodifiedDate = _super.lastmodifiedDate;

//inherited
public final StringPath name = _super.name;

public final com.apress.springpersistence.audiomanager.core.domain.components.
QPersonName personName;

//inherited
public final SimplePath<java.net.URL> sameAs = _super.sameAs;

public final StringPath telephone = createString("telephone");

//inherited
public final SimplePath<java.net.URL> url = _super.url;

//inherited
public final NumberPath<Integer> version = _super.version;

public QPerson(String variable) {
    this(Person.class, forVariable(variable), INITS);
}

public QPerson(Path<? extends Person> path) {
    this(path.getType(), path.getMetadata(), path.getMetadata().isRoot() ?
    INITS : PathInits.DEFAULT);
}

public QPerson(PathMetadata<?> metadata) {
    this(metadata, metadata.isRoot() ? INITS : PathInits.DEFAULT);
}

public QPerson(PathMetadata<?> metadata, PathInits inits) {
    this(Person.class, metadata, inits);
}
```

```
public QPerson(Class<? extends Person> type, PathMetadata<?> metadata, PathInits inits) {
    super(type, metadata, inits);
    this.fullName = inits.isInitialized("fullName") ? new com.apress.springpersistence.
    audiomanager.core.domain.components.QPersonName(forProperty("fullName")) : null;
    this.personName = inits.isInitialized("personName") ? new com.apress.
    springpersistence.audiomanager.core.domain.components.QPersonName(forProperty
    ("personName")) : null;
}

}
```

Note that the properties defined in the Person domain entity are all accounted for in this query class, but they are defined as type StringPath, NumberPath, EnumPath, and so forth. These properties provide the necessary features to express intuitive and type-safe queries.

Integrating QueryDSL with Spring

Now that we have integrated QueryDSL into our project, we now need to modify our DAO classes so that we can take advantage of this framework within our Repository layer. Let's take a look at our PersonRepository interface and make the necessary changes for integrating QueryDSL:

```
public interface PersonRepository extends CrudRepository<Person, String>, QueryDslPredicate
Executor<Person> {
}
```

Notice that this interface looks almost identical to the previous version:

```
public interface PersonRepository extends CrudRepository<Person, String {
}
```

In fact, the only thing that we added to this interface was to have our PersonRepository interface also extend QueryDslPredicateExecutor<Person>.

With this simple addition, we suddenly have a bunch of new methods that we can leverage:

```
T findOne(Predicate predicate);

Iterable<T> findAll(Predicate predicate);

Iterable<T> findAll(Predicate predicate, Sort sort);

Iterable<T> findAll(Predicate predicate, OrderSpecifier<?>... orders);

Iterable<T> findAll(OrderSpecifier<?>... orders);

Page<T> findAll(Predicate predicate, Pageable pageable);

long count(Predicate predicate);

boolean exists(Predicate predicate);
```

Notice that just about all of these methods take a `Predicate` parameter. The `Predicate` type is a key component of QueryDSL. You can define a predicate by utilizing the newly generated query classes. To illustrate an example, let's define a `PersonService` and add a method that allows us to search for a person by name or email:

```
@Service
public class PersonService {

    PersonRepository personRepository;

    @Autowired
    public void setPersonRepository(PersonRepository personRepository) {
        this.setPersonRepository(personRepository);
    }

    @Transactional(readOnly = true)
    public Iterable<Person> findPeopleByName(String nameOrEmail) {
        Predicate searchPredicate = QPerson.person.personName.fullName.containsIgnoreCase
        (nameOrEmail).or(QPerson.person.email.equalsIgnoreCase(nameOrEmail));

        return personRepository.findAll(searchPredicate);
    }

}
```

■ **Note**   Services is discussed in more detail later in this book.

In the preceding example, note that we first define a Predicate variable with utilizes our QPerson query class to create the necessary constraints around our query. In this case, we reference our Person entity's personName.name (remember that personName is actually an embedded type called PersonName, which includes properties such as firstName, lastName, etc.). Within each query class property, we have numerous methods provided by QueryDSL to help define our query. In this case, we used containsIgnoreCase so that we can find any Person entities that have a name that contains the search term. We also added a second condition by utilizing the or method. The second part of our Predicate looks for an exact, case-insensitive match on the Person.email property.

Once we define our predicate, we pass it to the PersonRepository.findAll(Predicate predicate) method, which we enable by having the PersonRepository interface extend QueryDslPredicateExecutor, as described earlier.

There is certainly much more to learn about QueryDSL, including join and fetch operations, and numerous other powerful querying features. You can learn more about this excellent framework at www.querydsl.com.

Summary

Frameworks like Spring and Hibernate provide a means to solve complex enterprise challenges. The critical difference between EJB 2.0 and frameworks like Spring and Hibernate is that this complexity is an option that you can elect to utilize, rather than an integral component of the framework architecture that you are forced to embrace.

In this chapter, you took a stroll down memory lane to see how persistence has evolved in the Java ecosystem. You now have a firmer understanding of the terminology and the distinctions between specifications and implementations. You learned that you can have an application that uses many permutations of specifications and implementations. For instance, you can build a single application that uses EJB 3.0 for a distributed component-based architecture, with JPA for persistence powered by Hibernate as the JPA implementation. You also got a feel for the domain model and DAO structure that underpins our art gallery example application. Finally, you learned quite a lot about setting up a JPA application in a Spring environment. You are now armed with enough information to get a JPA application working.

In the next chapter, we'll continue building the domain model for our art gallery application.

CHAPTER 5

Domain Model Fundamentals

The domain model is the foundation upon which a persistence tier is constructed. Each domain class defines the properties to be persisted to the database, as well as the relationships between one class and another. This rich object-oriented structure is not easily translated to the relational world of databases. Hibernate provides the required mechanism to help address this impedance mismatch between these two realms.

Mapping is the process through which you provide hints to Hibernate regarding how the properties and references in your domain classes are translated to tables, fields, and associations in your database. When Hibernate first appeared on the scene, developers used XML (called .hbm.xml files) to specify a domain model's mapping rules. With the release of the JPA specification came a series of annotations that can be applied to your domain classes, providing similar types of hints to the XML mapping files. However, because annotations can benefit from some of Java's core features, such as type safety, annotations provide a more intuitive and efficient approach for defining your mappings, compared to the old-school XML approach.

One of Hibernate's strengths is the ease with which developers can begin building a persistence tier. The first step is usually to define your domain model using simple JavaBeans (or POJOs). In the previous chapter, we introduced several core classes that compose the root of our application's domain model. In this chapter, we will build on this foundation, introducing some additional classes.

Understanding Associations

In Chapter 4, we introduced our AudioManager application domain model and created the Person entity. In addition to the Person class, we will need several other key entities in our domain model in order to represent the other elements our application will manage, such as media files, reviews, comments, and ratings.

The entity that is responsible for managing the persistence and querying of media files is the CreativeWork class. A CreativeWork naturally contains multiple comments to allow for an unlimited number of site visitors to add their own comments about the particular media or audio file they are viewing. Although a CreativeWork may contain many Comment instances, a given Comment can reference only a single CreativeWork, as typically a comment is intended to relate to a particular piece of content within the AudioManager application. The association between a CreativeWork and its Comment instances is best described as a *one-to-many* relationship. Inversely, the relationship between a Comment and its associated CreativeWork is known as a *many-to-one* association. Because each entity is able to reference the other, the association is considered *bidirectional*. If one entity is able to reference another entity, but the inverse is not true, this is considered a *unidirectional* association.

Whether you should use unidirectional or bidirectional associations depends on your application. However, if you don't have a specific requirement to use bidirectional associations, it is easier to stick with a unidirectional approach, because bidirectional associations can require circular references and may end up complicating marshaling or serialization implementations.

© Paul Fisher and Brian D. Murphy 2016
P. Fisher and B.D. Murphy, *Spring Persistence with Hibernate*, DOI 10.1007/978-1-4842-0268-5_5

It's always important to consider the way in which the domain model and its relationships are translated into a database schema, even when ORM abstractions often handle these details for us. The CreativeWork and Comment association require two tables: a Media_Object table and a Comment table. However, when we explore how to model polymorphic relationships, we will see how a domain model hierarchy can be represented across multiple tables (which, of course, increases the number of tables involved in this simple example).

A CreativeWork instance is then associated with a Comment through a foreign key reference to the Media_Object table from within the Comment table, as illustrated in Figure 5-1.

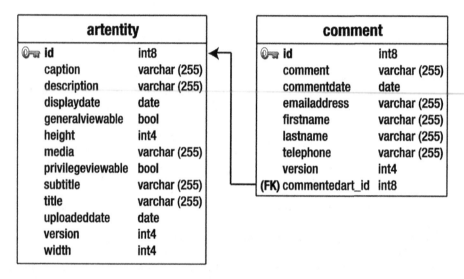

Figure 5-1. *The relationship between the MediaObject and Comment tables*

Our AudioManager application also requires a Category class to represent a category into which a particular CreativeWork may be placed (to help organize media and audio into logical groups). Each Category may contain more than one CreativeWork instance. Similarly, each CreativeWork may be placed into multiple Category entities. This type of association is normally referred to as *many-to-many*. The many-to-many association is a bit more complicated than the one-to-many relationship. The best way to model this type of relationship in the database is to use a *join table*. A join table simply contains foreign keys from the two related tables, allowing rows in the two tables to be associated with each other. Figure 5-2 illustrates this relationship.

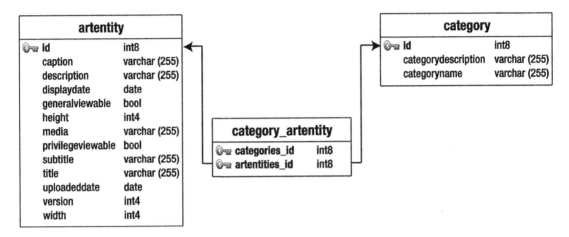

Figure 5-2. *The relationship between the MediaObject and Category tables*

Although it is important to have a clear understanding of your domain model's table structure, Hibernate can take care of creating these database-specific details for you. Instead, you need to focus on the definition of the classes and the way they relate to each other from an object-oriented standpoint.

Developers have different philosophies on the best way to go about defining a Hibernate domain model. Some developers believe it is best to define a database schema first, and then create the classes to match the database structure. Obviously, there is no wrong way (provided your application works reliably) to go about this process. However, in our experience, we have achieved the best results by defining the Hibernate mappings first, allowing us to consider the Java classes and the database table structure in tandem.

Building the Domain Model

We've already described a few of our sample application's core entities, along with their corresponding associations. Now that we've considered how these entities are represented in the database, let's start building our Java classes. Let's first define the Comment class:

```java
@Entity
public class Comment extends AbstractPersistable<Long> {

    @ManyToOne
    private CreativeWork creativeWork;

    @Basic
    private String content;

    @Version
    private Integer version;

    public String getContent() {
        return content;
    }
}
```

```java
    public void setContent(String content) {
        this.content = content;
    }

    public Integer getVersion() {
        return version;
    }

    public void setVersion(Integer version) {
        this.version = version;
    }

    public CreativeWork getCreativeWork() {
        return creativeWork;
    }

    public void setCreativeWork(CreativeWork creativeWork) {
        this.creativeWork = creativeWork;
    }

}
```

Next, let's define the CreativeWork class:

```java
@Entity
@Inheritance(strategy= InheritanceType.JOINED)
public class CreativeWork extends Thing {

    private String headline;
    private String alternativeHeadline;

    @ManyToOne
    private Person author;
    @OneToMany
    private Set<Comment> comments = new HashSet<Comment>();

    public boolean addComment(Comment comment) {
        comment.setCreativeWork(this);
        return this.getComments().add(comment);
    }

    @ManyToMany(mappedBy = "creativeWorks")
    private Set<Category> categories = new HashSet<Category>();

    @Temporal(TemporalType.DATE)
    private Date datePublished;

    private URL discussionUrl;

    private String genre;

    private Boolean isFamilyFriendly;
```

```java
private String keywords;
private URL license;

@ManyToOne
private Organization publisher; //Organization
@OneToMany
private Set<Review> reviews = new HashSet<Review>();

@Column(length = 4000, nullable = true)
@Basic(fetch = FetchType.LAZY)
@Lob()
private String text;

@org.hibernate.validator.constraints.URL
private URL thumbnail;
@ManyToOne
private Duration timeRequired;

public Boolean getFamilyFriendly() {
    return isFamilyFriendly;
}

public void setFamilyFriendly(Boolean familyFriendly) {
    isFamilyFriendly = familyFriendly;
}

public Organization getPublisher() {
    return publisher;
}

public void setPublisher(Organization publisher) {
    this.publisher = publisher;
}

public String getAlternativeHeadline() {
    return alternativeHeadline;
}

public void setAlternativeHeadline(String alternativeHeadline) {
    this.alternativeHeadline = alternativeHeadline;
}

public Person getAuthor() {
    return author;
}

public void setAuthor(Person author) {
    this.author = author;
}

public Set<Comment> getComments() {
    return comments;
}
```

```java
public void setComments(SortedSet<Comment> comments) {
    this.comments = comments;
}

public Integer getCommentCount() {
    return this.comments.size();
}

public Date getDatePublished() {
    return datePublished;
}

public void setDatePublished(Date datePublished) {
    this.datePublished = datePublished;
}

public URL getDiscussionUrl() {
    return discussionUrl;
}

public void setDiscussionUrl(URL discussionUrl) {
    this.discussionUrl = discussionUrl;
}

public String getGenre() {
    return genre;
}

public void setGenre(String genre) {
    this.genre = genre;
}

public String getHeadline() {
    return headline;
}

public void setHeadline(String headline) {
    this.headline = headline;
}

public String getKeywords() {
    return keywords;
}

public void setKeywords(String keywords) {
    this.keywords = keywords;
}

public URL getLicense() {
    return license;
}
```

```java
    public void setLicense(URL license) {
        this.license = license;
    }

    public void setComments(Set<Comment> comments) {
        this.comments = comments;
    }

    public Set<Review> getReviews() {
        return reviews;
    }

    public void setReviews(Set<Review> reviews) {
        this.reviews = reviews;
    }

    public boolean addReview(Review review) {
        return this.getReviews().add(review);
    }

    public String getText() {
        return text;
    }

    public void setText(String text) {
        this.text = text;
    }

    public URL getThumbnail() {
        return thumbnail;
    }

    public void setThumbnail(URL thumbnail) {
        this.thumbnail = thumbnail;
    }

    public Duration getTimeRequired() {
        return timeRequired;
    }

    public void setTimeRequired(Duration timeRequired) {
        this.timeRequired = timeRequired;
    }

    public Set<Category> getCategories() {
        return categories;
    }

    public void setCategories(Set<Category> categories) {
        this.categories = categories;
    }
}
```

■ **Note**   As mentioned earlier, the domain objects in these code listings extend the `AbstractPersistable` base class. This base class provides some boilerplate functionality that is useful for all of our entity classes, including the definition of each entity's identifier.

We've omitted some of the redundant getters and setters to conserve space. However, you'll immediately recognize that we're essentially defining a JavaBean or POJO. There is no reference to Hibernate dependencies, and although we extend from the AbstractPersistable class (or one of its subclasses), this isn't actually necessary.

We have defined the properties that we need to persist in the database along with their respective getters and setters. As well as the appropriate getters and setters, we have also added an addComment (`Comment comment`) method on the CreativeWork class. This is a convenience method and best practice for managing bidirectional associations, since it is important that references be set on both sides of the association. In the addComment(`Comment comment`) method, we ensure that the specified comment parameter is added to the `CreativeWork`'s comment collection and that the `Comment`'s creativeWork property properly references the `CreativeWork` instance to which the comment relates. We strongly recommend creating this type of "association management" method on one side of the relationship to ensure that both sides of a bidirectional relationship are properly set.

Our Comment domain entity also has the @ManyToOne annotation. This tells Hibernate that the creativeWork property will have a many-to-one association to the `CreativeWork` table. From a database perspective, specifying a @ManyToOne annotation on the Comment field will add a foreign key field on our Comment table to the `CreativeWork` table. This also demonstrates some of the advantages of using Hibernate to architect both your domain model and your database schema. If Hibernate is used to generate your schema, it will also create foreign key constraints for your associations to ensure the referential integrity of your database is not compromised.

Polymorphism in JPA

Our CreativeWork class extends the Thing parent class. Our Thing class then extends the AbstractPersistable base class, from which most of our entities also extend. We will discuss polymorphism in a bit more detail later in this chapter, but it's important to point out that one feature of JPA that comes in handy when many of your entities all share some of the same core properties (and, therefore, database columns) is the MappedSuperclass. A MappedSuperclass does not have its own table in the database. Instead, any class extended from a MappedSuperclass inherits all of the database fields defined by the MappedSuperclass. This can be an effective tool for reducing redundancy in your entity classes. In our AudioManager application, several entities, including the CreativeWork class, extend from the Thing class. Thing includes several integral properties that are useful for most of our entities, such as createdDate, lastModifiedDate (to keep track of when an entity was first inserted or last updated), a version number (which is useful for optimistic locking), and URL, name, and description fields. Let's take a look at the Thing class to get a better sense of what it provides:

```
@MappedSuperclass
public class Thing extends AbstractPersistable<Long> {

    @org.hibernate.validator.constraints.URL
    private URL url;
    private URL additionalType;
    private String alternateName;
```

```java
@Column(length = 255)
private String description;

@Column(length=255)
private String name;

@org.hibernate.validator.constraints.URL
private URL sameAs;

@Version
private Integer version;

@Temporal(TemporalType.TIMESTAMP)
private Date createdDate = new Date();
@Temporal(TemporalType.TIMESTAMP)
private Date lastmodifiedDate = new Date();

public URL getAdditionalType() {
    return additionalType;
}

public void setAdditionalType(URL additionalType) {
    this.additionalType = additionalType;
}

public String getAlternateName() {
    return alternateName;
}

public void setAlternateName(String alternateName) {
    this.alternateName = alternateName;
}

public String getDescription() {
    return description;
}

public void setDescription(String description) {
    this.description = description;
}

public String getName() {
    return name;
}

public void setName(String name) {
    this.name = name;
}

public URL getSameAs() {
    return sameAs;
}
```

```java
    public void setSameAs(URL sameAs) {
        this.sameAs = sameAs;
    }

    public URL getUrl() {
        return url;
    }

    public void setUrl(URL url) {
        this.url = url;
    }

    public Integer getVersion() {
        return version;
    }

    public void setVersion(Integer version) {
        this.version = version;
    }

    public Date getCreatedDate() {
        return createdDate;
    }

    public void setCreatedDate(Date createdDate) {
        this.createdDate = createdDate;
    }

    public Date getLastmodifiedDate() {
        return lastmodifiedDate;
    }

    public void setLastmodifiedDate(Date lastmodifiedDate) {
        this.lastmodifiedDate = lastmodifiedDate;
    }
}
```

Note that the @MappedSuperclass annotation is at the top of the Thing class, rather than the typical @Entity annotation. This tells Hibernate that we intend to have this class serve as a parent class for other entities, and that its properties are included in the respective database tables to which any of its subclasses maps.

Convention over Configuration

The simplicity of Hibernate's annotation support stems from using sensible defaults, as well as Hibernate's ability to infer associations and database field types by considering the Java type of each JavaBean property. When mappings are defined in XML, we must explicitly delineate the details of each property and association. With Hibernate, because annotations are embedded into code, we have the benefit of drawing hints from the code itself, which dramatically simplifies configuration efforts.

As you learned in Chapter 4, the key annotation for Hibernate persistence is @Entity. This annotation tells Hibernate that we intend to persist this class. If we were following the XML mapping approach, we would then need to define each field explicitly in the hbm.xml mapping file. With Hibernate annotations, it is necessary to define only the details that don't conform to Hibernate's default behavior.

Hibernate looks at each property's Java type and its name, and use this metadata to define a column's field type and field name, respectively. The default behavior is to assume that all POJO properties are persistable, but you can also specify this behavior explicitly by using the @Basic annotation. Using @Basic also provides you with a way to customize various persistence-related aspects, such as whether a particular property should be lazily loaded. If you don't want certain fields persisted, you need to specify that these properties are transient using the @Transient annotation.

■ **Note**   Hibernate offers control over fetching associations, allowing related entities to be lazily loaded—only when needed, rather than when the originating object is loaded from the database. This has dramatic performance benefits (if used properly), but can also degrade performance if you're not careful. We'll be covering lazy loading in more detail when we cover querying strategies later in this book.

In addition to the @Transient and @Basic annotations, you can also use the @Temporal annotation for controlling the way date or time-based properties are mapped to the database. In our Comment class, we specify the following to declare that a Date property be persisted in the database as a timestamp:

```
@Temporal(TemporalType.TIMESTAMP)
public Date getCreatedDate() {
    return this.createdDate;
}
```

This concept of sensible defaults, or *convention over configuration*, really reduces the amount of coding required to get a domain model up and running. And Hibernate's annotation support provides ample flexibility to override any of the default behavior, should you be so inclined. For instance, if we wanted to define a table name for our Comment class that is different from the Java class name, we could accomplish this feat by using the @Table annotation:

```
@Table(name = "HOGWASH")
class Comment {
    . . . (Methods Omitted)
}
```

Similarly, we can require that the comment property maps to the column commentText by using the @Column annotation:

```
@Column(name = "commentText")
public String getComment() {
    return this.commentText;
}
```

This level of customization is very useful, but most of the time is unnecessary and redundant (unless you are mapping your domain model to a legacy database).

■ **Note**   You should have a very good reason for creating column names that don't follow a consistent naming convention. The @Column annotation provides you with the flexibility to map any column name to any Java property, but this flexibility should be applied judiciously. If you feel the need to map a Java property to a column of a different name, you may want to consider defining your own naming strategy, which defines a consistent pattern for mapping Java properties to column names (as well as class names to tables, etc.). You can define the rules for how your database fields and tables map to Java properties and classes by extending Hibernate's ImprovedNamingStrategy class. Spring Boot also ships with a class called SpringNamingStrategy, which adds improvements to Hibernate's ImprovedNamingStrategy.

Managing Entity Identifiers

Hibernate annotation support does require that you define a primary key and all of your JavaBean's associations. Because most of our entities extend from Spring's AbstractPersistable class, we delegate to it for specifying the @Id annotation. By using AbstractPersistable, we simply need to specify the generic type of our identifier when extending this class. For example, we specify that we want to use a java.lang. Long identifier in the following snippet:

public class Thing **extends** AbstractPersistable<Long> { . . .

If we choose not to utilize the AbstractPersistable base class, we can specify our ID mapping directly by placing the @Id annotation above the property that maps to our table's primary key. Typically, we would add the @Id annotation above a getId() method. This annotation tells Hibernate that the id property of our class is the identifier (or primary key) for our entity. Let's look at a concrete example:

```
@Id
@GeneratedValue(strategy = GenerationType.AUTO)
private Long id;
```

Below the @Id annotation is the @GeneratedValue annotation, which specifies the way in which a given instance's identifier is created. The default is AUTO, and in our example, Hibernate will use this identifier-generation strategy (since we haven't defined a strategy at all). AUTO looks at the underlying database to make the decision as to how identifiers should be created. The options are to use a sequence, an identity column, or a special table for generating new IDs. If you wanted to override the default behavior and use a sequence, your @GeneratedValue annotation might look like this:

```
@GeneratedValue(strategy=GenerationType.SEQUENCE, generator="COMMENT_ID_SEQ")
```

This creates a sequence named COMMENT_ID_SEQ for generating new IDs for the Comment table. Hibernate offers many more options for a domain class's identifier, including UUID-based generation or simply allowing your application to assign identifiers directly.

■ **Note**   When using the AUTO mode for ID generation, Hibernate picks the ideal strategy based on the database that you are using. However, for many databases, Hibernate ends up creating a single sequence to use across all of your tables. This can get a bit messy. We have often found that creating explicit sequences for each table is a little cleaner. If your domain model has some complexity to it, we recommend specifying a different sequence for each table or class.

Using Cascading Options to Establish Data Relationships

Associations within a domain model represent how different domain entities relate to one another. Often, these relationships can be expressed in layman's terms as *parent-child relationships*, meaning that one entity owns or encapsulates a collection of another entity. Within the database, associations are represented through table joins, but there is no clear analogue for representing the more hierarchical relationships that we have within Java. This is where Hibernate comes in. Cascading options help to establish parent-child relationships, or more precisely, the rules for how operations such as save and delete that are applied to one entity should *cascade* to associated entities. This concept is often referred to as *transitive persistence*.

For example, within our AudioManager application, we would assert that CreativeWork owns a collection of Comment instances. This is logical since a Comment is *attached* to a particular CreativeWork instance. An end user can post a comment about a particular media file, and this comment is typically relevant only to the media element about which it was posted. Furthermore, if a CreativeWork instance is deleted, it doesn't make sense to keep its related Comment instances around anymore. In essence, comments are children of a CreativeWork.

Since comments can be considered children of a CreativeWork, we can assert that a save operation invoked on a CreativeWork should also cascade to any added or updated Comment instances associated to that CreativeWork instance. Additionally, should a CreativeWork be deleted, we would want the delete action to cascade to any associated Comment instances. We can represent these cascading rules using the following annotation:

```
@OneToMany(orphanRemoval = true, cascade = { javax.persistence.CascadeType.ALL })
public Set<Comment> getComments() {
    return comments;
}
```

In this case, we are setting orphanRemoval to true, which ensures that any dereferenced comments are also deleted. We also specify a CascadeType of SAVE_UPDATE, which ensures that save and update operations invoked on a CreativeWork instance are passed along to child Comment instances as well.

Adding Second-Level Caching

Hibernate allows entities, as well as association collections (a group of comments) to be implicitly cached. With caching enabled, Hibernate first tries to find an entity or collection in the cache before trying to query the database. Since loading data from the cache is far less expensive than performing a database operation, caching is another effective strategy for improving application performance.

Hibernate integrates with several caching frameworks, such as Ehcache, and provides a CacheManager interface if you want to add your own caching solution. Once integrated, caching happens implicitly, without requiring any additional coding, other than specifying caching rules for each entity and collection.

To get basic caching enabled on our domain model, we can add the following annotation to each domain entity, as well as its corresponding collections, to ensure they are appropriately cached:

```
@Entity
@Cache(usage = CacheConcurrencyStrategy.NONSTRICT_READ_WRITE)
public class ArtEntity implements Serializable {

    . . . Methods Omitted . . .

    @OneToMany(orphanRemoval = true, cascade = { javax.persistence.CascadeType.ALL })
    @Cache(usage = CacheConcurrencyStrategy.NONSTRICT_READ_WRITE)
    public Set<Comment> getComments() {
        return comments;
    }
```

```
    public void setComments(Set<Comment> comments) {
        this.comments = comments;
    }

    . . . Methods Omitted . . .

}
```

Specifying a read-write caching strategy ensures that Hibernate will invalidate the cache whenever a particular domain instance is updated. This prevents stale data from being stored in the cache.

There are three types of caching options for Hibernate: domain, collection, and query. Domain and collection caching are demonstrated in the preceding example, as we have specified the @Cache annotation for the top-level domain entity as well as for the comments association.

Caching details should be adjusted using the configuration file appropriate for the caching implementation you have selected. In the case of Ehcache, you can configure specifics, such as the time-to-live and cache size on a domain-by-domain basis within the ehcache.xml file.

We will cover caching strategies in more detail in Chapter 9.

Using Polymorphism with Hibernate

For our gallery application, we require a few more classes to help provide the persistence details for all of the gallery's functionality. As a quick recap, here is an overview of our domain model, as it currently stands:

- Person: Represents an administrative user or a registered user of our application.

- Category: Organizes collections of media elements into logical groups.

- CreativeWork: Represents a media element in the application and contains metadata about the image, as well as its location.

- Comment: Represents an individual comment that relates to a particular CreativeWork instance.

Our CreativeWork class represents basic metadata about a media element, but what if we need to store a media file in different resolutions or bit-depths, such as thumbnails and high-resolution versions for images and low-quality and high-quality versions of audio files? We could certainly insert additional fields into our CreativeWork class, but Hibernate provides a cleaner solution.

ORM solutions like Hibernate go far beyond mapping database fields to domain model instances. Object-oriented concepts, such as polymorphism, are also enabled by Hibernate and are an effective means for establishing a hierarchy of domain objects that share a set of core properties and functionality.

Rather than store an image path directly within our CreativeWork class, let's instead refactor this data into a separate base class called ArtData. We will then create three subclasses that each extend the MediaData class (and therefore share its properties) but are tailored to represent a particular type of image. We will define the following four new domain classes:

- MediaData: The bulk of the properties will be stored here, since it is the base class.

- MediaData_Default: This class will be used to represent the standard representation of an image or audio file within the app's listing pages.

- MediaData_Low: This class will be used to represent thumbnails.

- MediaData_High: This class will persist a high-resolution version of the image, suitable for archival purposes or for zoomed-in views.

■ **Note**   We won't include the entire source code for our domain model here. You can download the example code for this chapter if you would like to follow along.

Hibernate provides four different options for implementing polymorphism:

- *Implicit polymorphism*: This option uses the Java inheritance structure without requiring these structural details to affect the database schema. In other words, using implicit polymorphism, you are able to query a parent class, and Hibernate will issue select queries for all tables within the specified Java class hierarchy. While this strategy allows you to leverage the polymorphic structure inherent in your Java classes without affecting the database, these types of queries can be a bit inefficient, as Hibernate must do a lot more heavy lifting to translate distinct tables into a coherent class hierarchy, without being able to effectively leverage the database. The other polymorphic strategies rely on the database to some degree to delineate the associations between classes in the Java hierarchy.

- *Table-per-hierarchy*: This option combines all the properties of a class hierarchy into a single table, using a *discriminator field* to help determine which Java type is represented by each row in the database. A discriminator is simply a table column, the value of which is used to specify to which class that particular row should be associated. The advantage of this approach is that all the necessary fields for any class within the hierarchy are included in a single table, without requiring the overhead of a database join. The disadvantage is that the design is not very normalized, and for any given type, there will likely be fields that will not be utilized. This can impose limitations on your database schema, such as preventing you from being able to specify not-null constraints. Since field requirements will differ between classes in the hierarchy and they are all shared within a single table, you must simplify the schema down to the lowest common denominator.

- *Table-per-subclass*: Using this option, each Java class in the hierarchy is represented by a different table. Properties related to the parent class are persisted to a single table. The specific properties unique to each subclass are stored within their own database tables. A particular subclass in the hierarchy is then represented through a join between the parent table and the subclass table. The advantage of this approach is that the design is clean and normalized, since shared properties are stored in a single parent table and only subclass-specific attributes are sequestered into their own subclass tables. However, although cleaner from a relational database modeling perspective, you should consider the performance hit incurred by the necessity of joining tables together.

- *Table-per-concrete-class*: This option requires that every Java class that is not declared as abstract be represented by its own table. Subclasses are not implemented as joins between multiple tables. Instead, all the properties of each class—including those properties inherited from a parent class—are persisted to their own table. This obviously requires a bit of redundancy, as the same fields across a class hierarchy is present in each mapped table. However, Hibernate can implement polymorphic queries more efficiently by leveraging SQL unions across all tables mapped to a particular class hierarchy. The downside is the increased verbosity and redundancy in your database schema. Furthermore, Hibernate imposes limitations on the ID-generation strategy used by tables mapped with this polymorphic approach.

The option to use really depends on your domain model. If there isn't too much disparity across classes within your class hierarchy, then the table-per-hierarchy option probably makes the most sense. This is the strategy that we employ in our case.

Let's take a look at the base MediaData entity:

```
@Entity
@Inheritance(strategy = InheritanceType.SINGLE_TABLE)
@DiscriminatorColumn(discriminatorType = DiscriminatorType.STRING)
@DiscriminatorValue("GENERIC")
public class MediaData extends AbstractPersistable<Long> {

    private byte[] data;

    public MediaData() {
    }

    public MediaData(byte[] data) {
        this.data = data;
    }

    public byte[] getData() {
        return data;
    }

    public void setData(byte[] data) {
        this.data = data;
    }

}
```

Much of this class should look familiar. You will notice the standard JavaBean conventions, as well as the core Hibernate annotations. Let's focus on the annotations that enable the inheritance in our model.

The @Inheritance annotation tells Hibernate that we want to use inheritance and that we are defining our base class.

```
@Inheritance(strategy=InheritanceType.SINGLE_TABLE)
```

We are also specifying that we intend to use the table-per-hierarchy strategy (meaning that we want to persist all the fields in the entire hierarchy within a single table).

The @DiscriminatorColumn annotation provides Hibernate with the details about our discriminator. As mentioned earlier, the discriminator provides Hibernate with the clues it needs to infer to which Java type a particular database row corresponds. In our example, we are defining our discriminator column to be a String type. We could also use a char or an Integer.

Last, we define the discriminator value that each type will use through the @DiscriminatorValue annotation. In the case of the MediaData base class, we specify a value of GENERIC. So, for each MediaData instance that is persisted to the database, Hibernate will set the discriminator column to a value of GENERIC.

Next, we must define the classes that extend from our MediaData base class. Each class is fairly similar to one another in our scenario, but inheritance provides a clean way to classify the different types of images within our gallery application. Furthermore, this approach also provides future extension points, should we need to define additional metadata that only relates to a particular image type, such as a thumbnail aspect ratio or archival details for our MediaDataStorage class.

Here's our MediaDataLow class:

```
@Entity
@DiscriminatorValue("LOW")
public class MediaDataLow extends MediaData {

    public MediaDataLow(byte[] data) {
        this.setData(data);
    }

    public MediaDataLow() {
    }

}
```

This is a fairly straightforward class. Notice, however, that we've set a discriminator value of THUMBNAIL. Let's look at our CreativeWork class with all of our refactorings applied:

```
@Entity
@Inheritance(strategy= InheritanceType.JOINED)
public class CreativeWork extends Thing {

    private String headline;
    private String alternativeHeadline;

    @ManyToOne
    private Person author;
    @OneToMany
    private Set<Comment> comments = new HashSet<Comment>();

    public boolean addComment(Comment comment) {
        comment.setCreativeWork(this);
        return this.getComments().add(comment);
    }

    @ManyToMany(mappedBy = "creativeWorks")
    private Set<Category> categories = new HashSet<Category>();

    @OneToOne(cascade = CascadeType.ALL)
    @JoinColumn()
    private MediaData mediaData;
    @OneToOne(cascade = CascadeType.ALL)
    @JoinColumn()
    private MediaDataLow mediaDataLow;
    @OneToOne(cascade = CascadeType.ALL)
    @JoinColumn()
    private MediaDataHigh mediaDataHigh;

    @Temporal(TemporalType.DATE)
    private Date datePublished;
```

```java
private URL discussionUrl;

private String genre;

private Boolean isFamilyFriendly;

private String keywords;
private URL license;

@ManyToOne
private Organization publisher; //Organization
@OneToMany
private Set<Review> reviews = new HashSet<Review>();

@Column(length = 4000, nullable = true)
@Basic(fetch = FetchType.LAZY)
@Lob()
private String text;

@org.hibernate.validator.constraints.URL
private URL thumbnail;
@ManyToOne
private Duration timeRequired;

public Boolean getFamilyFriendly() {
    return isFamilyFriendly;
}

public void setFamilyFriendly(Boolean familyFriendly) {
    isFamilyFriendly = familyFriendly;
}

public Organization getPublisher() {
    return publisher;
}

public void setPublisher(Organization publisher) {
    this.publisher = publisher;
}

public String getAlternativeHeadline() {
    return alternativeHeadline;
}

public void setAlternativeHeadline(String alternativeHeadline) {
    this.alternativeHeadline = alternativeHeadline;
}

public Person getAuthor() {
    return author;
}
```

```java
public void setAuthor(Person author) {
    this.author = author;
}

public Set<Comment> getComments() {
    return comments;
}

public void setComments(SortedSet<Comment> comments) {
    this.comments = comments;
}

public Integer getCommentCount() {
    return this.comments.size();
}

public Date getDatePublished() {
    return datePublished;
}

public void setDatePublished(Date datePublished) {
    this.datePublished = datePublished;
}

public URL getDiscussionUrl() {
    return discussionUrl;
}

public void setDiscussionUrl(URL discussionUrl) {
    this.discussionUrl = discussionUrl;
}

public String getGenre() {
    return genre;
}

public void setGenre(String genre) {
    this.genre = genre;
}

public String getHeadline() {
    return headline;
}

public void setHeadline(String headline) {
    this.headline = headline;
}

public String getKeywords() {
    return keywords;
}
```

```java
public void setKeywords(String keywords) {
    this.keywords = keywords;
}

public URL getLicense() {
    return license;
}

public void setLicense(URL license) {
    this.license = license;
}

public void setComments(Set<Comment> comments) {
    this.comments = comments;
}

public Set<Review> getReviews() {
    return reviews;
}

public void setReviews(Set<Review> reviews) {
    this.reviews = reviews;
}

public boolean addReview(Review review) {
    return this.getReviews().add(review);
}

public String getText() {
    return text;
}

public void setText(String text) {
    this.text = text;
}

public URL getThumbnail() {
    return thumbnail;
}

public void setThumbnail(URL thumbnail) {
    this.thumbnail = thumbnail;
}

public Duration getTimeRequired() {
    return timeRequired;
}
```

```java
    public void setTimeRequired(Duration timeRequired) {
        this.timeRequired = timeRequired;
    }

    public Set<Category> getCategories() {
        return categories;
    }

    public void setCategories(Set<Category> categories) {
        this.categories = categories;
    }

    public MediaData getMediaData() {
        return mediaData;
    }

    public void setMediaData(MediaData mediaData) {
        this.mediaData = mediaData;
    }

    public MediaDataLow getMediaDataLow() {
        return mediaDataLow;
    }

    public void setMediaDataLow(MediaDataLow mediaDataLow) {
        this.mediaDataLow = mediaDataLow;
    }

    public MediaDataHigh getMediaDataHigh() {
        return mediaDataHigh;
    }

    public void setMediaDataHigh(MediaDataHigh mediaDataHigh) {
        this.mediaDataHigh = mediaDataHigh;
    }
}
```

Notice that we have now defined a few one-to-one relationships for our thumbnailPicture, galleryPicture, and storagePicture properties. To simplify our code, we defined three separate one-to-one associations. However, we could have also chosen to put all the ArtData entities into a single collection, with a generic type of the ArtData base class. Since each image type is represented by a different subclass, it would be easy to differentiate between the different image types.

Also, notice that we have defined a many-to-many association to the Category class for the categories property. We have added the mappedBy hint here to indicate that the inverse side of this relationship is referenced by the artEntities property in the Comment class. For bidirectional many-to-many associations, we need to tell Hibernate which side of the collection is the owner. By adding the mappedBy attribute to the Comment class, we are asserting that the Category class owns the relationship.

OVERRIDING EQUALS AND HASHCODE

In simple scenarios, Hibernate is able to maintain entity equivalence without requiring any special changes to the domain objects themselves. However, if your application requires that you add entities to Java collections, such as `java.util.Set`, or you plan to work with detached entities, you will probably need to override the default `equals()` and `hashCode()` methods for your domain objects.

Hibernate is able to maintain entity equivalence only within a single EntityManager scope. If you attempt to reattach a detached entity, Hibernate is no longer able to make the same guarantees. The way to resolve this problem is to override `equals()` and `hashCode()` for each of your domain objects, providing equality rules that are reflective of its identity within the database.

The simplest approach is to use an entity's identifier to determine equality and generate its hash code. However, if you are planning to use a generated identifier strategy, this can have negative implications. When an object is first created, it will have a default null identifier. If you attempt to add this newly created entity to a `java.util.Set` and then later save this instance, the invocation of `EntityManager.save()` will trigger an identifier to be generated for the entity in question. However, because you have based `equals` and `hashCode` on the object's identifier, you will run into a situation where the `hashCode` for the object suddenly changes. This change breaks the contract for many of the Java collection types, such as `Set`, and could lead to unexpected behavior in your application.

There are two options to get around this problem:

- Don't use a generated identifier strategy (and instead assign an entity identifier when the domain object is first instantiated)

- Base `equals()` and `hashCode()` on business equality, rather than row equality

Using an assigned identifier strategy isn't too difficult, but can impose some limitations on your application. Generally, the recommended approach is to generate `equals()` and `hashCode()` using the values of key properties of a domain object—specifically, properties that define an object's uniqueness from a business logic perspective.

Here is an example of a customized `equals` and `hashCode` for the `Category` domain object:

```
@Override
public boolean equals(Object o) {
    if (this == o) return true;
    if (!(o instanceof Category)) return false;

    Category category = (Category) o;
    if (categoryName != null ?
            !categoryName.equals(category.categoryName) : category.categoryName
            != null) {
        return false;
    } else {
        return true;
    }
}
```

```
@Override
public int hashCode() {
    return categoryName != null ? categoryName.hashCode() : 0;
}
```

Summary

In this chapter, we introduced the fundamentals for defining a domain model with Hibernate. You learned about the mapping process and how you can use annotations to provide Hibernate with the appropriate clues to effectively map your object-oriented domain classes to your relational database.

We also examined association mapping, differentiating between the various cardinality options Hibernate provides. These details—such as whether to use many-to-many or one-to-many associations—have a significant impact on your domain model design, as well as the resultant database schema. Furthermore, it is important to think carefully about whether an association should be unidirectional or bidirectional. While bidirectional associations are often necessary to simplify reference walking and access, this option can have consequences in terms of circular dependencies that may complicate marshaling implementations.

Hibernate provides a powerful feature called *cascading* that allows you to associate the operations applied to one entity with its children entities so that these operations cascade. This feature is useful for ensuring that child entities are kept in sync with the state and life cycle of their parent entities.

CHAPTER 6

■ ■ ■

Transaction Management

Database transactions help you group a set of operations into a single unit of work. All operations either succeed or fail as a group.

Spring's powerful and flexible transaction support is another factor responsible for the framework's success and popularity. Before Spring, complex or declarative transactional features typically required that an organization use EJB, along with a heavyweight JEE container. Using aspect-oriented programming (AOP) techniques, Spring helped democratize enterprise-level transactional support, allowing developers to cleanly apply transactional rules to their code whether they were using a full-fledged Java EE application server, a lighter-weight web container, or even a stand-alone unit test.

Not only did Spring help to obviate the need for a heavyweight container, but it also provided a generalized abstraction for transaction management. It no longer mattered whether you were using Hibernate transactions, local database transactions, or even the Java Transaction API (JTA), which allows for distributed transactions across multiple datasources. In much the same way that Spring provides a generic DataAccessException hierarchy, Spring's abstraction for transaction management and demarcation helps to simplify and decouple transactional specifics from application code and business logic.

Much of the popularity of EJB stemmed from its transactional support. EJB provided a way to specify transactional rules via configuration, preventing these details from adding too much complexity to data access code. By leveraging its AOP features, Spring is able to offer similar flexibility, but without the overhead of a heavy EJB container or the addition of complexity or features that an organization doesn't require.

Using Spring, transactional rules can be consolidated into configuration so that code need not be muddied with these types of concerns. Switching between a Java EE application server using a JTA datasource and a simple unit test using a local datasource is just a matter of modifying the Spring configuration—no code needs to be altered. Spring can leverage some of the advanced features offered by JTA when employing a JTA transaction manager. The key benefit, however, is that Spring provides a transactional programming model that is consistent; whether you need to have transactions span across multiple datasources (a feature offered by JTA) or across a single datasource, the way that you define these transactional concerns will always be the same.

In rare cases where you actually want to define transactional rules for your application programmatically, Spring offers a means for accomplishing this as well. You could just rely on Hibernate's transactional programming model, but by leveraging Spring's abstractions, you reduce your coupling to Hibernate by basing your persistence code on generalized APIs. This might come in handy if you decide to move away from Hibernate in the future, or (more likely) if your persistence layer utilizes both Hibernate and JDBC.

Spring allows you to control how transactions are performed at a per-method level. Transaction management can be applied via XML configuration or using annotations. In this chapter, we will demonstrate both approaches. However, we recommend using annotations, as this strategy is the most intuitive and allows transactional metadata to be embedded directly within a service layer class or interface.

© Paul Fisher and Brian D. Murphy 2016
P. Fisher and B.D. Murphy, *Spring Persistence with Hibernate*, DOI 10.1007/978-1-4842-0268-5_6

The Joy of ACID

Before we begin adding transactions to our application using Spring, let's discuss some of the fundamental and theoretical concepts. There's quite a bit to know about transactions, but the most important details to understand are encapsulated in the acronym ACID, which defines the four core requirements of a transaction:

- *Atomicity* specifies that all operations within a single transaction must complete together or not at all. In other words, a transaction allows multiple database operations to be applied together. In the event of an error, the entire set of operations is rolled back.

- *Consistency* refers to the requirement that transactions must transition a database from one consistent state to another consistent state. A successful transaction cannot leave the database in a state that violates the integrity constraints of the database or the schema. In other words, transactions must comply with database constraints and referential integrity rules during every insert, update, or delete before a transaction may be committed.

- *Isolation* defines the rules about how one running transaction affects or interacts with other concurrently running transactions. The isolation strategy used on a transaction is very important. If the chosen isolation level is too loose, hard-to-find bugs can be introduced, which may adversely impact the integrity of your data. If your isolation level is too high, however, you run the risk of slowing down your application or deadlocking your database. This setting is both application server and database server dependent. While there are technically eight isolation levels, generally you will only need to concern yourself with the four that are defined by the ANSI/ISO SQL standard. You should also note that the default isolation level varies quite a bit amongst DBMS vendors.

- *Durability* ensures that once a transaction is committed, the changes will not be lost and should survive database failures.

In this chapter, we will cover the fundamentals of ACID transactions, as well as how to declaratively apply transactions using Spring. These concepts will undoubtedly prove useful for any type of application development, and they might come in handy during your next job interview! (Although we recommend waiting for these topics to come up themselves in the context of a job interview—we do not recommend starting out by confessing your love for ACID.)

ACID can be perceived as a bit trippy, but it has a way of keeping your data safe and it will definitely maintain your sanity when dealing with persistence.

So why should you care about ACID? It's important to understand the available rules and options of database behavior so that you can effectively leverage these features in the context of your application.

These details are critical for controlling how a group of operations are applied to a database or how concurrent database modifications can affect each other. Improper transaction management can also adversely affect performance in an enterprise application.

Understanding Isolation Levels

The four isolation levels that you'll encounter in practice, listed from least isolated to most isolated, are Read Uncommitted, Read Committed, Repeatable Read, and Serializable. These isolation levels also have an impact on concurrency. The least stringent isolation level allows for the highest number of concurrent database operations, while the most stringent are all but guaranteed to slow down your systems. Figure 6-1 highlights the ramifications of each isolation level including a demonstration of the correlation between isolation level and concurrency.

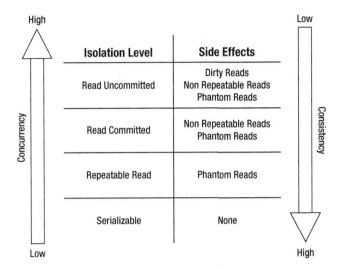

Figure 6-1. *Isolation levels mandate tradeoffs between consistency and concurrency*

In order to explain the side effects outlined in Figure 6-1, consider the following scenario in our application:

1. Paul opens a database transaction, T1, and SELECTs everything from the Playlist table.

2. Brian initiates a separate transaction, T2, to DELETE a playlist from the Playlist table.

3. Brian, still in his same T2 transaction, UPDATEs a record in the Playlist table, correcting a typo.

4. Paul, still in his same T1 transaction, SELECTs all playlists in the Playlist table a second time.

5. Brian's transaction, T2, COMMITs.

6. Mary initiates a new transaction, T3, and INSERTs a new playlist to the Playlist table.

7. Paul, still in his same T1 transaction, SELECTs all playlists in the Playlist table a third time.

8. Mary's T3 transaction COMMITs.

9. Paul, still in his same T1 transaction, SELECTs all playlists in the Playlist table a fourth time.

10. Paul's transaction, T1, finally COMMITs.

What should Paul see in step 4? What about steps 7 and 9? Your database vendor will have default behaviors defined, but it's important to know that you have absolute control over the outcome by choosing the isolation level you prefer for your transactions. Let's take a look at how the four isolation levels impact this scenario.

Serializable

The easiest isolation level to understand is serializable, which mandates complete isolation. If we choose serializable as our isolation level, Paul will never see any of Brian's or Mary's changes until Paul begins a new transaction. From Paul's perspective, the database remains completely consistent and there are no side effects; Paul will see the same results for his query all four times because they all take place within a single transaction that is insulated from any other modifications. That sounds pretty ideal, right? So what more is there to talk about? Unfortunately, there is a lot of overhead associated with this setting. Using serializable vastly reduces the number of concurrent operations that may occur and can result in nasty performance problems involving database locks. As such, the serializable isolation level should be used sparingly, when the use case really requires absolute consistency and it's acceptable to risk the chance that concurrent transactions may be forced to abort with an error.

Repeatable Read

Relaxing isolation a bit by employing the repeatable read isolation level in our scenario would allow Paul to see any inserts that are committed, but not updates or deletes. In order to guarantee that rereads of the same row stay consistent, the underlying database ordinarily implement either row-level, shared read locks, or multiversioning. Under this isolation level setting, Paul would not see Brian's update or delete at any point in the scenario. However, Paul will see Mary's insert at step 9 after she has committed her transaction. This side effect—in which newly inserted and committed rows are visible to Paul's query (step 9) that weren't visible earlier (steps 4 and 7) within a single transaction (T1)—is known as a *phantom read*.

Read Committed

Read committed is the default isolation level used by most RDBMS vendors, including Oracle and PostgreSQL. This isolation level states that a transaction may read only data that has been committed in the database. When choosing read committed, Paul will see any changes made by Brian or Mary after their respective transactions have completed and been committed. This provides some data consistency while still delivering high concurrency. As with the repeatable read isolation level, Paul is still susceptible to phantom reads. As was the case with the repeatable read isolation level, Paul's query at step 9 will return a new record that wasn't visible earlier in his transaction. When choosing read committed, Paul is also exposed to a second type of side effect; a *nonrepeatable read*. A nonrepeatable read occurs when rereads of the same row return different data within the same transaction. This becomes possible after Brian's update and delete are committed in step 5. Unlike what happened under the serializable or repeatable read isolation levels, these row-level modifications become visible to Paul in step 7, even though Paul read these two rows earlier and he's still in the context of his first and only transaction, T1. When in doubt, choose the read committed isolation level, because, despite some of these trade-offs, it offers a good balance between performance and isolation.

Read Uncommitted

On the polar opposite end of the spectrum from serializable is the read uncommitted isolation level. If we employ read uncommitted for our scenario, there will be no transactional isolation whatsoever. Consequently, Paul's first three identical queries will all return different results. If Mary's commit in step 8 succeeds, Paul's fourth query will return the same results as his third query.

At step 4, Paul sees Brian's typo correction (SQL UPDATE) as well as the removal he performed (SQL DELETE) before Brian's transaction commits. This third side effect is commonly referred to as a *dirty read* because Paul is reading in *tentative data*. If Brian's commit fails at step 5, forcing his transaction to roll back, the data Paul is looking at will be rendered completely inaccurate. Reading in Mary's insert at step 7, prior to her commit, is also representative of a dirty read because that too represents tentative data.

Choosing the read uncommitted isolation level exposes you to all three of the possible side effects. Intuitively, this represents a strategy that is not ideal. However, there is a silver lining with the read uncommitted isolation level. Because this isolation level offers the highest degree of concurrency, one can expect each of Paul, Brian, and Mary's SQL operations to be incredibly fast. You might adopt this isolation level when you need to emphasize speed and you're confident that your application can cope with the side effects. As with serializable, read uncommitted should only be considered for fringe use cases.

Controlling ACID Reflux

Transactions define how and when data is committed to a database. They are indispensable in grouping persistence logic together, ensuring that all methods complete successfully or that the database is rolled back to its previous state. For most operations, you also need to be concerned with transactional details, ensuring that transactions are started at the beginning of an operation and are either committed or rolled back when the operation completes. Spring enables these features through three core concepts:

- *Platform transaction management* refers to Spring's abstraction for handling commits and rollbacks. Frameworks like Hibernate and JPA have their own transaction implementations. Furthermore, transactions typically operate differently in a testing environment than within an EJB server. Spring's platform transaction management abstraction hides these details, allowing developers to specify transactional rules in a consistent manner.

- *Declarative transaction management* allows developers to specify the transactional requirements for a particular method through metadata or configuration. Obviously, the code to set up, commit, and roll back a given transaction is still being executed. However, these details may be separated from the code itself and externalized into configuration files or annotations.

- *Programmatic transaction management* explicitly controls the transaction through code. Spring provides a `TransactionTemplate` class that can greatly simplify the code required to apply transactional semantics to a given method. However, this approach requires that transactional details be blended with business logic and requires your code to directly interact with the Spring APIs.

We'll look at each of these types of transaction in the following sections.

Platform Transaction Management

Spring offers several `TransactionManager` implementations, each of which fills the role of (drum roll please) managing transactions. `TransactionManager` instances typically extend the `AbstractPlatformTransactionManager` class, which in turn implements the `PlatformTransactionManager` interface. These classes form the foundation of Spring's transactional support, and provide the know-how to access, initiate, rollback, and commit transactions. The interface looks like this:

```
public interface PlatformTransactionManager {
    TransactionStatus getTransaction(TransactionDefinition definition)
        throws TransactionException;

    void commit(TransactionStatus status) throws TransactionException;

    void rollback(TransactionStatus status) throws TransactionException;
}
```

There are quite a few `TransactionManager` implementations. For our purposes, we are predominantly interested in Spring's ORM-based `TransactionManager` implementations: `HibernateTransactionManager` and `JpaTransactionManager`.

You'll even find `TransactionManager` implementations for JTA used by EJB. JTA is typically used to enable transactions to span across multiple databases and even disparate technologies, such as Java Message Service (JMS). These include the generic `JtaTransactionManager` and implementations for specific EJB servers like `OC4JJtaTransactionManager` for Oracle's server, `WebLogicJtaTransactionManager` for BEA's server, and `WebSphereUowTransactionManager` for IBM's server.

By adding the `<tx:jta-transaction-manager/>` XML tag to your Spring configuration, you can empower Spring to determine which JTA transaction manager to use, based on runtime information, so that you don't need to explicitly reference the platform-specific details in your configuration.

You might have noticed the `TransactionStatus` and `TransactionDefinition` interfaces that are part of the `PlatformTransactionManager` interface. You rarely need to use these interfaces yourself. They are set up by Spring's declarative transaction management (discussed in the next section), but they are still worth knowing about, as these details help to explain how Spring's transactional features work under the hood.

> `TransactionStatus`: Encapsulates key information related to an actively running transaction, such as whether a new transaction has been created and whether the transaction should be rolled back or committed. It also allows the transaction to be marked as `Rollback-Only`. Setting a running transaction to be `Rollback-Only` tells the transaction system that the transaction should be rolled back. For example, in the event of an error condition, you might write code to call `setRollbackOnly()` on a `TransactionStatus` instance, which will ensure that the actively running transaction is rolled back.

> `TransactionDefinition`: Defines the ACID properties we talked about earlier, including details such as the isolation rules for the transaction, whether your transaction will perform any writes (or is read-only), how long the transaction is allowed to run before timing out, and how to handle transaction propagation.

We will learn more about how these classes are used later in this chapter when we discuss programmatic transaction management.

Declarative Transaction Management

Declarative programming employs metadata to define the requirements for a particular set of application logic, rather than coding the steps that define this behavior directly. Typically, you use declarative programming within the context of a framework, which is designed to analyze the metadata in order to tailor its behavior accordingly. Using declarative transaction management, therefore, implies that you define the rules or attributes that compose your transactions' behavior, rather than interspersing this logic directly in your code. As you can probably guess, Spring applies these cross-cutting concerns to your code by levering its excellent AOP support. However, because transactions are such a prevalent and critical feature, the AOP details are a bit abstracted to provide a clearer and more transaction-specific approach.

Spring has a fantastic annotation-driven approach for transaction management. An alternative is to use an XML-driven strategy based on Spring configuration. We will discuss both of these approaches, beginning with annotation-based transaction management, since you have seen examples of this in earlier chapters.

Transactional Annotations

Using the @Transactional annotation, you can set some transactional behavior and attributes.

Propagation defines the transactional behavior for the specified method. This setting determines whether a new transaction should always be created, whether a nested transaction should be created, or even if no transaction should be created at all. Here are the Propagation values you can use in Spring:

- REQUIRED: If there's a transaction, support it; otherwise, create a new one.

- SUPPORTS: If there's a transaction, it will be supported, but this is not a requirement.

- MANDATORY: There must be a transaction; otherwise, throw an exception.

- REQUIRES_NEW: Create a new transaction and suspend the current one if it exists.

- NOT_SUPPORTED: Execute the code within the "transactionalized" method non-transactionally and suspend the current transaction.

- NEVER: Throw an exception if a transaction exists.

- NESTED: Perform a nested transaction if a transaction exists; otherwise, create a new transaction. Nested transactions offer a way to provide more granular transactional behavior, allowing a group of inner transactions to be executed. This can be useful, for example, for cases in which some nested transactions may get rolled back, but without aborting the entire operation.

Isolation is the "I" in ACID, and defines how a running transaction affects (and is affected by) other database processes occurring within the application. The following are settings to control isolation behavior for a given transaction:

- DEFAULT: Let the datastore define the isolation level.

- READ_UNCOMMITTED: This isolation level allows changes made by other running transactions to be read by the actively running transaction, even when the other transactions have not committed. In other words, this setting enables dirty reads.

- READ_COMMITTED: Dirty reads are not allowed, but phantom reads are. Only changes applied by successfully committed transactions are visible.

- REPEATABLE_READ: Indicates that dirty reads and nonrepeatable reads are prevented but phantom reads may occur.

- SERIALIZABLE: Indicates that dirty reads, nonrepeatable reads and phantom reads are prevented.

Spring also provides a way to specify some of the fundamental attributes of a transaction. For instance, you can use the readOnly attribute to indicate whether a transaction is read-only (as opposed to a transaction in which inserts or updates are performed). A readOnly value of true ensures that the method performs only read operations.

The timeout attribute defines how long a transaction can live without committing or rolling back. If the timeout for a running transaction elapses without the transaction completing, Spring automatically rolls back the transaction.

Spring's transactional support provides a means to specify how a transaction should behave if an exception is thrown. For example, we could specify that whenever an InvalidAudioFormatException is thrown from a method within our AudioCaptureService, the currently running transaction should be rolled back. Spring provides the attributes rollbackFor and rollbackForClassName to enable this behavior. This setting allows you to specify an array of either classes or class names (depending on the setting used) of exceptions that, when thrown, will trigger the currently executing transaction to be automatically rolled back.

Similarly, you may specify the inverse of this behavior (which exceptions should not trigger a rollback) through the use of the noRollbackForClass and noRollbackForClassName attributes. These options work the same way as rollbackFor and rollbackForClassName, but prevent a transaction from being rolled back if one of the specified exception classes is thrown while this transaction is being executed.

Armed with a clearer understanding of some of the configuration options for Spring transactions, let's take a look at how we can specify the transactional semantics for our service class. To keep things simple, we will examine a scaled-back version of our AudioService class.

```
@Service
public class AudioService {

    private AudioObjectRepository audioObjectRepository;

    public AudioObjectRepository getAudioObjectRepository() {
        return audioObjectRepository;
    }

    @Autowired
    public void setAudioObjectRepository(AudioObjectRepository audioObjectRepository) {
        this.audioObjectRepository = audioObjectRepository;
    }

    @Transactional(rollbackFor=InvalidAudioFormatException.class,
            readOnly=false,
            timeout=30,
            propagation= Propagation.SUPPORTS,
            isolation= Isolation.DEFAULT)
    public void saveAudio(AudioObject entity) throws InvalidAudioFormatException {
        this.getAudioObjectRepository().save(entity);
    }

}
```

Here, we define a transactional service method that specifies a timeout of 30 seconds, and automatically rolls back if an InvalidAudioFormatException is thrown. Notice that we have also configured the transaction to be writable (readOnly is set to false).

Now that we've configured the details of our transaction, we need to set up our transaction manager. As noted earlier, Spring provides a PlatformTransactionManager interface, along with a set of implementations for use with different persistence strategies. For global transactions that span multiple datasources, we would need to use Spring's JTA support. For our example, we will use Spring's JpaTransactionManager. Our JpaConfig.java configuration class should be updated to reflect the following (the important bits for transaction support have been bolded):

```
package com.apress.springpersistence.audiomanager.core.config;

import org.springframework.beans.factory.annotation.Autowired;
import org.springframework.boot.autoconfigure.jdbc.DataSourceBuilder;
import org.springframework.boot.autoconfigure.jdbc.DataSourceProperties;
import org.springframework.boot.context.properties.ConfigurationProperties;
import org.springframework.boot.context.properties.EnableConfigurationProperties;
```

```java
import org.springframework.context.annotation.Bean;
import org.springframework.context.annotation.Configuration;
import org.springframework.context.annotation.Profile;
import org.springframework.context.annotation.PropertySource;
import org.springframework.core.env.Environment;
import org.springframework.data.jpa.repository.config.EnableJpaRepositories;
import org.springframework.orm.jpa.JpaTransactionManager;
import org.springframework.orm.jpa.JpaVendorAdapter;
import org.springframework.orm.jpa.LocalContainerEntityManagerFactoryBean;
import org.springframework.orm.jpa.vendor.HibernateJpaDialect;
import org.springframework.orm.jpa.vendor.HibernateJpaVendorAdapter;
import org.springframework.transaction.annotation.EnableTransactionManagement;
import org.springframework.transaction.jta.JtaTransactionManager;

import javax.persistence.EntityManager;
import javax.persistence.EntityManagerFactory;
import javax.sql.DataSource;
import javax.transaction.SystemException;
import java.util.Properties;

@Configuration
//@Profile("jpa")
@EnableJpaRepositories("com.apress.springpersistence.audiomanager.core")
@EnableConfigurationProperties
@EnableTransactionManagement
@PropertySource("classpath:jpa.properties")
public class JpaConfig {

    @Autowired
    private Environment environment;

    @Autowired
    private DataSourceConfigurationPropertiesBean dataSourceProperties;

    @Bean
    @ConfigurationProperties(prefix = "datasource")
    public DataSource dataSource() {
        DataSourceBuilder factory = DataSourceBuilder
                .create(this.getClass().getClassLoader())
                .driverClassName(this.dataSourceProperties.getDriverClassName())
                .url(this.dataSourceProperties.getUrl())
                .username(this.dataSourceProperties.getUsername())
                .password(this.dataSourceProperties.getPassword());
        return factory.build();
    }

    @Bean
    public LocalContainerEntityManagerFactoryBean entityManagerFactory() {
        LocalContainerEntityManagerFactoryBean lef = new LocalContainerEntityManagerFactoryBean();
        lef.setDataSource(dataSource());
```

```java
        lef.setJpaVendorAdapter(new HibernateJpaVendorAdapter());
        lef.setJpaDialect(new HibernateJpaDialect());
        String[] packages = environment.getProperty("jpa.entities.package").split(",");
        lef.setPackagesToScan(packages);

        Properties props = new Properties();
        props.put("hibernate.show_sql", "true");
        props.put("hibernate.format_sql", "true");
        props.put("hibernate.ejb.naming_strategy", "org.hibernate.cfg.ImprovedNamingStrategy");
        props.put("hibernate.connection.charSet", "UTF-8");
        props.put("hibernate.current_session_context_class", "jta");
        props.put("hibernate.archive.autodetection", "class");
        props.put("hibernate.transaction.manager_lookup_class", "org.springframework.orm.
        hibernate4.HibernateTransactionManager");
        props.put("hibernate.dialect", environment.getProperty("jpa.dialect"));
        props.put("hibernate.hbm2ddl.auto", environment.getProperty("jpa.hibernate.create.
        strategy"));
        lef.setJpaProperties(props);

        lef.afterPropertiesSet();

        return lef;
    }

    @Bean
    public JpaVendorAdapter jpaVendorAdapter() {
        HibernateJpaVendorAdapter hibernateJpaVendorAdapter = new HibernateJpaVendorAdapter();
        hibernateJpaVendorAdapter.setShowSql(false);
        hibernateJpaVendorAdapter.setGenerateDdl(true);
        hibernateJpaVendorAdapter.setDatabasePlatform(environment.getProperty("jpa.dialect"));

        return hibernateJpaVendorAdapter;
    }

    @Bean
    public JpaTransactionManager jpaTransactionManager(EntityManagerFactory entityManagerFactory) {
        JpaTransactionManager transactionManager = new JpaTransactionManager();
        transactionManager.setEntityManagerFactory(entityManagerFactory);
        return transactionManager;
    }

}
```

The configuration in this example specifies the necessary configuration for setting up our JPA
DataSource and our PlatformTransactionManager. We are using Spring's JpaTransactionManager, but
the way in which we are able to declaratively configure transactions would not be different if we decide to
create a JDBC implementation, or even if we required global transactions via JTA. Spring allows us to use a
consistent strategy for specifying transactions, regardless of the underlying implementation details.

In the event that we don't want to leverage Spring's code-based configuration strategy, we can also turn to the more classical XML-based approach for configuring our JPA DataSource and PlatformTransactionManager:

```xml
<?xml version="1.0" encoding="UTF-8" standalone="no"?>
<beans xmlns="http://www.springframework.org/schema/beans"
       xmlns:aop="http://www.springframework.org/schema/aop"
       xmlns:context="http://www.springframework.org/schema/context"
       xmlns:tx="http://www.springframework.org/schema/tx"
       xmlns:xsi="http://www.w3.org/2001/XMLSchema-instance"
       xsi:schemaLocation="http://www.springframework.org/schema/aop
       http://www.springframework.org/schema/aop/spring-aop-4.1.xsd
       http://www.springframework.org/schema/beans http://www.springframework.org/schema/
       beans/spring-beans-4.1.xsd
       http://www.springframework.org/schema/context http://www.springframework.org/schema/
       context/spring-context-4.1.xsd
       http://www.springframework.org/schema/tx http://www.springframework.org/schema/tx/
       spring-tx-4.1.xsd">
    <!--
        This will automatically locate any and all property files you have
        within your classpath, provided they fall under the META-INF/spring
        directory. The located property files are parsed and their values can
        then be used within application context files in the form of
        ${propertyKey}.
    -->
    <context:property-placeholder
            ignore-resource-not-found="true"
            location="classpath*:*.properties"/>

    <!-- post-processors -->
    <context:annotation-config/>

    <context:spring-configured/>

    <context:component-scan base-package="com.apress.springpersistence">
        <context:exclude-filter expression="org.springframework.stereotype.Controller"
        type="annotation"/>
    </context:component-scan>
    <bean class="org.apache.commons.dbcp.BasicDataSource" destroy-method="close"
    id="dataSource">
        <property name="driverClassName" value="${jpa.driver.classname}"/>
        <property name="url" value="${database.url}"/>
        <property name="username" value="${database.username}"/>
        <property name="password" value="${database.password}"/>
        <property name="testOnBorrow" value="true"/>
        <property name="testOnReturn" value="true"/>
        <property name="testWhileIdle" value="true"/>
        <property name="timeBetweenEvictionRunsMillis" value="1800000"/>
        <property name="numTestsPerEvictionRun" value="3"/>
        <property name="minEvictableIdleTimeMillis" value="1800000"/>
        <property name="validationQuery" value="SELECT 1;"/>
    </bean>
```

```
<!--Use Hibernate SessionFactory instead? -->
<bean class="org.springframework.orm.jpa.JpaTransactionManager" id="transactionManager">
    <property name="entityManagerFactory" ref="entityManagerFactory"/>
</bean>
<tx:annotation-driven />

<bean class="org.springframework.orm.jpa.LocalContainerEntityManagerFactoryBean"
id="entityManagerFactory">
    <property name="persistenceUnitName" value="persistenceUnit"/>
    <property name="dataSource" ref="dataSource"/>
    <property name="persistenceXmlLocation" value="classpath:META-INF/persistence.
    xml"></property>
    <property name="jpaDialect" value="${jpa.dialect}"/>
    <property name="packagesToScan" value="${jpa.entities.package}"/>
</bean>

</beans>
```

Notice the `tx:annotation-driven` bean that Spring includes in its `tx` namespace. This XML snippet is necessary to enable the usage of our `@Transactional` annotations. Without it, Spring would not enable transactions for our `ArtEntityService`. The `tx:annotation-driven` annotation supports the following options and features:

- `transaction-manager`: This supplies the name of the bean used for the transaction manager. As we'll discuss later in this chapter, when we demonstrate using two datasources, you can have more than one transaction manager in your Spring application context.

- `mode`: This specifies the type of proxying mechanism you want. You have a choice of `proxy` to use Spring proxying or `aspectj` to use AspectJ, an industrial-strength AOP framework. The default is `proxy`.

- `proxy-target-class`: By default, Spring creates a Java proxy object, and attaches only the interfaces that the object implements. For example, if you have a `PersonDaoJPA` class that implements a `PersonDao` interface, the proxying process will create an object that implements `PersonDao`, adds on the implementation of your transactional semantics, and passes the request on to your implementation. If the class doesn't implement any interfaces or you need the proxy to extend the class and not just its interfaces, Spring will then use the Code Generation Library (CGLIB) open source byte-code manipulation framework to perform the proxying. The CGLIB approach does have a limitation: you need to put the transactional annotations on the class itself, not on the interface.

- `order`: There are plenty of other frameworks that take advantage of proxying, but to use them, you may need to explicitly order the transactional and other proxying mechanisms. Lower order numbers are processed first.

Declarative Transactions via XML

Rather than using the `@Transactional` annotation for applying transactional semantics, you can take a pure XML-driven approach. This approach is useful in cases where you prefer not to apply annotations, or you can't use annotations because you need to use JDK1.4 or you want to apply transactional semantics to a library that you can't change.

Coupling the tx:advice XML configuration with an XML-based AOP configuration makes for a synergistic combination. For example, you can use method names to automatically figure out what kind of transactionality you want to apply.

Here's an example that specifies that methods starting with save, update, and delete require a transaction, and everything else supports (but does not require) a read-only transaction:

```
<tx:advice id="txAdvice" >
    <tx:attributes>
        <tx:method name="save*" propagation="REQUIRED"/>
        <tx:method name="update*" propagation="REQUIRED"/>
        <tx:method name="delete*" propagation="REQUIRED"/>
        <tx:method name="*" propagation="SUPPORTS" read-only="true"/>
    </tx:attributes>
</tx:advice>
```

tx:advice does support a transaction-manager XML attribute, but by default, it uses the name transactionManager, just like tx:annotation-driven.

In addition to the flexible method name matching, the tx:method element has the same types of parameters as the @Transactional annotation. You can set values for propagation, isolation, timeout, read-only, rollback-for, and no-rollback-for. These tx:method XML attributes have the same values as their @Transactional counterparts.

One more detail needs to be added to this example in order to make it complete. You need to use Spring's AOP framework to define which beans require the advice. You can accomplish this by using the aop namespace in your Spring XML file. For example, if we wanted to apply the transactional advice to all of the classes that are in the com.apress.springpersistence.audiomanager.core.service package, we can add the following to our Spring XML file:

```
<aop:config>
    <aop:pointcut id="allServices"
                  expression="execution(*com.apress.springpersistence.audiomanager.core.
                  service .*.*(..))"/>
    <aop:advisor advice-ref="txAdvice" pointcut-ref="allServices"/>
</aop:config>
```

Spring AOP is pretty flexible, and even lets you use annotations to define the pointcut. If you want to apply txAdvice to any class that is annotated with @Transactional, you can change the allServices pointcut to this:

```
<aop:pointcut id="allServices"
              expression="@target(org.springframework.transaction.annotation.Transactional)"/>
```

You can even combine the two pointcut approaches, like so:

```
<aop:pointcut
    id="allServices"
    expression="execution(*com.apress.springpersistence.audiomanager.core.service .*.*(..)) &&
        @target(org.springframework.transaction.annotation.Transactional)"/>
```

Let's take a look at one more Spring AOP trick: using the bean name to define a pointcut. Here's how to apply a transaction to a bean named personService:

```
<aop:pointcut id="allServices" expression ="bean(personService)"/>
```

You can also use the asterisk (*) wildcard character to match against all beans that end with Service or Dao, as follows:

```
<aop:pointcut id="allServices" expression ="bean(*Service) || bean(*Dao)"/>
```

If applying complex AOP pointcuts to ACID transactions is still a bit too mind-altering for you, you'll find plenty of documentation out there.[1] However, the information you've gleaned here should give you a running start in understanding how to get your ACID transactions in order.

Programmatic Transaction Management

We can't think of many real-world use cases for working with programmatic transactions rather than leveraging Spring's simpler declarative transaction support. However, understanding programmatic transactions can prove helpful in comprehending the way in which Spring transactions work under the hood.

To demonstrate how programmatic transactions work, we will rework the AudioService example to use programmatic transactions, as follows;

```
public class AudioServiceImpl implements AudioService {

    private TransactionTemplate transactionTemplate;

    public AudioServiceImpl (PlatformTransactionManager transactionManager) {
        this.transactionTemplate = new TransactionTemplate(transactionManager);
    }

    public Object saveAudio (AudioObject audio) {
        return transactionTemplate.execute(
            new TransactionCallback() {
                public Object doInTransactionWithoutResult(TransactionStatus status) {
                    try {
                        this.getAudioObjectRepository().save(audio);
                    } catch (InvalidAudioFormatException e) {
                        status.setRollbackOnly();
                    }
                    return;
                }
            }
        );
    }

}
```

[1] If you would like to learn more about the huge and important field of transaction processing, consider reading *Transaction Processing: Concepts and Techniques* by Jim Gray and Andreas Reuter (Morgan Kaufmann, 1992); *Principles of Transaction Processing*, Second Edition, by Philip A. Bernstein and Eric Newcomer (Morgan Kaufmann, 2009); and *Pro JPA 2: Mastering the Java Persistence API* by Mike Keith and Merrick Schincariol (Apress, 2009).

In this snippet, we rely on constructor injection to provide a reference to our JpaTransactionManager (which is an implementation of the PlatformTransactionManager interface). Using transactionManager, we create an instance of TransactionTemplate, which we use to wrap our persistence behavior within the scope of a transaction.

The usage of the TransactionTemplate should look very familiar to you. This is a common Spring idiom, and works in a similar fashion to the HibernateTemplate we use within our DAO classes. The key difference here is that we are using the TransactionTemplate to handle the boilerplate process of transactions, rather than database connection setup and closing.

To wrap our persistence code within a transaction, we call the execute method on our transactionTemplate property, passing in an anonymous implementation of TransactionCallback as a parameter. In the example, our service method does not return a value, so we implement the method doInTransactionWithoutResult. However, if we needed to return a value from our transaction, we would instead use doInTransaction.

Within the scope of the TransactionCallback, we are calling the same persistence code that we used in our annotation-based example. We delegate to our audioObjectRepository to do the heavy lifting. Notice, however, that we catch the InvalidAudioFormatException, and should the exception get thrown, we use the TransactionStatus parameter to roll back the transaction.

This approach is not as clear or as elegant as using declarative transactions in Spring. Nevertheless, it is helpful to see how the various components fit together without relying on AOP to inject this behavior implicitly.

Transactional Examples

Now that we've covered the main transactional concepts, let's go through a couple of real-world scenarios. We'll look at a batch application and transactions involving two datasources.

Creating a Batch Application

Batch applications can be a bit of a drag, especially with ORM frameworks. Both the database and the ORM framework need to reserve valuable resources for each operation performed in a transaction. The database needs to keep locks on the tables that you've changed. The ORM, for a variety of reasons, needs to cache the objects that you've persisted and read from the database. The more operations a transaction executes, the more resources the ORM and database need to dedicate to it.

Let's start out with the following example, which updates a whole bunch of records:

```
@Transactional(readOnly = false, propagation = Propagation.SUPPORTS)
public void batchProcessAll() {
    int count = dao.getCount();
    // do your ACID business in a big for loop
}
```

Here, we're attempting to update all of the data in a single transaction. Depending on the amount of data and system resources, this may not be possible, or it may lead to degraded performance for our application. Instead, we may be able to find a way to define smaller units that can be committed, which will free up some of the resources utilized by the database and ORM framework. However, the process of committing the transaction consumes resources as well. If we commit too often, we'll probably decrease performance. There's a balance between committing too often and too little—for example, committing after a certain number of items have been processed.

We can create a method that processes *x* number of units and commits after it completes. It's actually quite simple to set this up. We'll choose 100 as an arbitrary number of *units of work*.

```
// no transaction on this method anymore
public void batchProcessAll() {
    int count = dao.getCount();
    for(int i=0; i<count; i+= 100) {
        doMyUnit(i, i+100);
    }
}
```

```
@Transactional(readOnly = false, propagation = Propagation.REQUIRES_NEW)
public void doMyUnit(int start, int finish) {
    // do your ACID business from the unit's
    // start to finish
    dao.flush();
}
```

Note the use of `Propagation.REQUIRES_NEW`. It tells Spring that a new transaction begins when the method is invoked and commits when the method completes. It's just that simple to create and commit a transaction. There are many variables, ranging from server capacity to application load, to be able to prescribe an ideal batch size, so determining the best size for your application will likely require some trial and error.

Using Two Datasources

Assume you have two databases, and you want to apply the right transactions to the right beans. You need to create two different `transactionManagers` that must be applied to the appropriate subsets of Spring beans. You can do that with some fancy AOP work.

Assume that you have already configured `transactionManager1` and `transactionManager2` beans. You'll need to start with the following XML:

```
<tx:advice id="txAdvice1" transaction-manager="transaction-manager1" >
    <tx:attributes>
        <tx:method name="save*" propagation="REQUIRED"/>
        <tx:method name="update*" propagation="REQUIRED"/>
        <tx:method name="delete*" propagation="REQUIRED"/>
        <tx:method name="*" propagation="SUPPORTS" read-only="true"/>
    </tx:attributes>
</tx:advice>
```

```
<tx:advice id="txAdvice2" transaction-manager="transaction-manager2" >
    <tx:attributes>
        <tx:method name="save*" propagation="REQUIRED"/>
        <tx:method name="update*" propagation="REQUIRED"/>
        <tx:method name="delete*" propagation="REQUIRED"/>
        <tx:method name="*" propagation="SUPPORTS" read-only="true"/>
    </tx:attributes>
</tx:advice>
```

```
<aop:config>
    <aop:advisor advice-ref="txAdvice1" pointcut-ref="allDatabaseOneBeans"/>
    <aop:advisor advice-ref="txAdvice2" pointcut-ref="allDatabaseTwoBeans"/>
    <!-- Add pointcuts here -->
</aop:config>
```

The `tx:advice` element tells Spring what needs to be done, and the `aop:config` element tells Spring where it needs to be done.

The question now is what beans should have which advice? Some beans need `txAdvice1`; others need `txAdvice2`; and others may need both. Thankfully, Spring AOP provides several mapping options. You might chose to organize your classes into packages that differentiate between the two datasources to which they relate and apply an expression pointcut, or you can devise logical bean names that clearly infer which advice to apply. You can also create our own annotations, `@Transaction1` and `@Transaction2` for example, and use the `expression="@target(...)"` approach.

Let's go through a quick bean name example. Imagine we have two datasources: `datasource1` and `datasource2`. Let's say that all of the `datasource1` beans have `ds1` as part of their bean name. For example, if `PersonDao` is intended to interface with `datasource1`, it would be called `ds1.personDao`. If `PersonService` depends on `personDao` as well as a DAO from `datasource2`, it should be called `ds1.ds2.personService`. Our pointcuts will look like the following:

```
<aop:pointcut id="allDatabaseOneBeans" expression ="bean(*ds1*)"/>
<aop:pointcut id="allDatabaseTwoBeans" expression ="bean(*ds2*)"/>
```

We've defined two pointcut expressions that utilize a bean-naming convention to properly infer which datasource and `transactionManager` to utilize for a given transaction.

Summary

In this chapter, you learned both the fundamentals and low-level details for managing database transactions with Spring. We explored two different avenues for applying transactions declaratively with Spring: via annotation and through both Java-based config as well as the more classical XML-based Spring configuration. It's also possible to utilize Spring's transaction management programmatically, through the use of the `TransactionTemplate`. However this approach couples transactional behavior with the application's business logic.

Understanding how transactions work, along with the available configuration options, is critical for developing and debugging multiuser applications. We discussed both simple and complex scenarios in this chapter, and we hope they give you a taste of what's possible when using Spring for transaction management.

Most importantly, Spring provides a consistent approach for applying transactional semantics to an application, no matter what the architecture or environment. This means that you can configure and code your application the same way, regardless of whether you're deploying to a Java EE app server using a JTA datasource or to a lightweight container with a local datasource. The difference is just a matter of configuration.

CHAPTER 7

Effective Testing

Automated testing, and unit testing in particular, is now universally regarded as a best practice for software development. A number of testing frameworks are available. There remains plenty of room to debate the merits of unit testing versus integration testing; whether to mock objects with frameworks like Mockito or to take a more classic approach with basic stubs; when to apply test-driven development (TDD); whether behavior-driven development (BDD) will become commonplace; and so on.

Throughout this book, we've highlighted several best practices, including layering your application and coding to interfaces. In this chapter, we'll demonstrate how these principles lend themselves to building solid test coverage with proper emphasis on exercising aspects of an application in isolation.

A code base that is broken down into layers so that each layer has a unique responsibility is much more testable than code that attempts to combine multiple aspects of functionality into a single class. Testable code is decoupled and divided into logical layers. Well-layered code is testable because it produces small, defined parts of an application's overall vision. By coding to interfaces and leveraging Spring's dependency-injection capabilities, you gain the ability to mock or stub one layer (such as the Repository layer) when you're testing the layer above it (in this case, the Service layer that uses repositories).

Dependency-injection frameworks like Spring are tremendously useful for testing because they make it relatively easy to instantiate classes directly, providing collaborators through code. With Spring in particular, you can automatically inject dependencies within your test classes simply by specifying the appropriate annotations. This allows you to construct an application context for your tests that uses configuration options that may differ quite a bit from your production setup. This flexibility enables you to test your code against a large number of potential inputs.

When it comes to verifying assertions of a persistence tier, it is important to verify the behavior of your Repository and Service classes, the configuration details and behavior of your domain classes, and even the collaboration and wiring of dependencies.

We will skim the surface of these strategies in this chapter, but it is important to keep in mind that an effective testing strategy should incorporate both unit and integration tests. Luckily, Spring helps to simplify the creation of both of these kinds of tests, as well as other forms of automated testing, such as functional testing with tools like Selenium.

Unit, Integration, and Functional Testing

Spring makes it easy to test specific parts of your code without relying on an application server or other infrastructural details. You can switch between different database implementations and datasources, or test your Repository classes in isolation by mocking these details.

Unit testing is an effective strategy for verifying that a particular class works properly in isolation. Assessing classes in isolation is very valuable, and there is no commensurate replacement for a good unit test. Writing an effective unit test involves the definition of assertions regarding the behavior of specific areas of a class in isolation. Good test coverage is related to which lines of code have their expected behavior verified.

© Paul Fisher and Brian D. Murphy 2016
P. Fisher and B.D. Murphy, *Spring Persistence with Hibernate*, DOI 10.1007/978-1-4842-0268-5_7

Unlike unit testing, *integration testing* typically verifies multiple components simultaneously, often by running the same implementation layers used within the production version of an application. For instance, a common practice for integration testing is to instantiate the Spring `ApplicationContext` to test a Repository implementation using an in-memory database along with the Spring/Hibernate abstractions. The advantage of this approach is that you are touching multiple components, ensuring that all the pieces are working together properly. The disadvantage is that it doesn't provide much granularity to ascertain whether a particular component works properly on its own.

Modern IDEs (Eclipse, IntelliJ IDEA, NetBeans, and many more) and other runtime environments (such as Maven and Gradle) know how to run both individual unit tests and test suites, which can include both unit and integration tests. It's common to use the notion of suites to strategically bundle tests together. For example, you might want a test suite of fast unit tests that are run on every commit and a different test suite composed of longer-running integration tests, which are done on some scheduled interval.

Functional tests are another strategy for verifying that your application is behaving properly. Functional tests provide the most high-level assessment of a code base, and typically require that an application run within a production environment container—for instance, using a servlet container.

Functional tests in a web application context usually involve a series of HTTP requests and then assertions as to the responses that should be returned. For example, a RESTful web service might include a battery of functional tests that verify the data that is returned when a chunk of XML is POSTed to a particular URL. Another type of functional test might verify certain HTML elements within a returned HTTP response, given a particular URL.

The downside of functional tests, especially as they relate to verifying HTML markup, is that they tend to be very brittle—meaning they are likely to break due to minor changes to the application. However, functional tests do have their place, and they are often an effective tool to verify basic assumptions regarding an application's behavior.

For a comprehensive testing strategy, you want to find the right balance of unit, integration, and functional tests. Figure 7-1 portrays our spin on the Test Automation Pyramid that was originally described by Mike Cohn in his book, *Succeeding with Agile* (Addison-Wesley Professional, 2009).

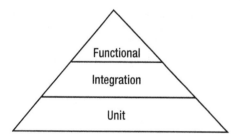

Figure 7-1. *The Testing Automation Pyramid*

The Test Automation Pyramid encourages you to favor more unit tests than integration tests, and more integration tests than functional tests to get the right mix of coverage and adaptability in your codebase. You want a small number of functional tests exercising your UI, a moderate amount of integration tests exercising your service layers, and as many unit tests as you can muster for your code base.

Using JUnit for Effective Testing

The two biggest unit-testing frameworks in the Java community at present are JUnit and TestNG. For our examples, we will use JUnit. JUnit 4's approach is highly annotation-based. The @Test annotation is all you need to add to define a test. To get started, we first need to add a new dependency on the spring-boot-starter-test in our pom.xml, like so:

```
<dependency>
    <groupId>org.springframework.boot</groupId>
    <artifactId>spring-boot-starter-test</artifactId>
    <scope>test</scope>
</dependency>
```

Doing so adds several libraries to our project's classpath, including JUnit for unit testing, Spring Test for integration testing Spring applications, Mockito for mocking expectations and behavior for objects, and the Hamcrest library, which provides a series of matcher objects that allow for advanced assertions.

■ **Note**   The scope for the spring-boot-starter-test is declared as test so that Maven knows that these additions should only be included during test compilation and test execution. When you run your application, or build an output archive for your project, these additional dependencies are included.

We'll dive deeper into all of these concepts as the chapter progresses. First, let's look at a trivially simple unit test that requires nothing more than JUnit. You'll see this test under src/test in our application:

```
package com.apress.springpersistence.test;

import org.junit.Test;
import org.junit.Assert;

public class TrivialJUnitTest {

    @Test
    public void testSimpleStuff() {
        String name = "SpringPersistenceWithHibernate";
        Assert.assertEquals("SpringPersistenceWithHibernate", name);
    }

}
```

To see the test in action, you can run the following Maven command in the root of our sample project:

```
mvn -Dtest=TrivialJUnitTest test
```

The –Dtest= flag tells Maven to execute a single named test. Alternatively, you might execute mvn test-compile to compile all of your tests, or simply mvn test to compile and execute all of the tests in a given project. The output will look something like this:

```
-----------------------------------------------------------
 T E S T S
-----------------------------------------------------------
Running com.apress.springpersistence.audiomanager.test.TrivialJUnitTest
Tests run: 1, Failures: 0, Errors: 0, Skipped: 0, Time elapsed: 0.057 sec - in com.apress.
springpersistence.audiomanager.test.TrivialJUnitTest

Results :

Tests run: 1, Failures: 0, Errors: 0, Skipped: 0
```

You can see that one test ran. Each method with a @Test annotation counts as a single test. You should strive to keep each test method as succinct as possible. Any time you find yourself wanting to test multiple things, or expressing many assertions in a single method, you should probably consider refactoring to break that single large method into multiple smaller tests.

There are two additional basic JUnit annotations that help define the life cycle of the test and make it easier to reuse common elements across test methods. You can run code immediately before and after each test method using the @Before and @After annotations. Guess which one comes before a test? You can also run code before and after all tests in a particular class using @BeforeClass and @AfterClass. (Note that the @BeforeClass method must be static.) There's also an @Ignore annotation that allows you to use a @Test annotation and not run a particular method.

Of course, the main point of a test is to set up a scenario and then verify a group of assertions. JUnit provides several built-in assertions, such as verifying that two values should be equal, a returned value is not null, and so on. You'll notice many of these annotations in the following example.

```java
package com.apress.springpersistence.test;

import org.junit.Test;
import org.junit.Ignore;
import org.junit.Assert;
import org.junit.Before;
import org.junit.BeforeClass;

public class SimpleJUnitTest {

    public static String staticName = null;
    public String memberName = null;

    @BeforeClass
    public static void initializeClass() {
        staticName = "Rod Johnson";
    }

    @Before
    public void initializeTest() {
        memberName = "Gavin King";
    }
```

```java
@Test
public void simpleEqualsAssertion() {
    Assert.assertEquals("Rod Johnson", staticName);
}

@Test
public void simpleBooleanAssertion() {
    Assert.assertFalse(staticName.equals(memberName));
}

@Test
@Ignore
public void dontTestThis() {
    // notice that this would fail without @Ignore
    Assert.assertEquals("Rod", memberName);
}

}
```

Now let's move beyond the basics and apply some tests to our application.

Unit Testing with Mocks

The tests in the previous examples are fairly simple because they don't have any dependencies on the Spring container or the implementations of other classes or components. Because our tests are isolated to a specific class, they qualify as unit tests. Most of the time, you'll need to go beyond such basic testing to simulate the effects of two or more classes interacting with each other. Integration tests are one way to achieve this, but that generally entails a fair amount of code and tight coupling of tests. An alternate strategy is to use *stubs* or *mocks*.

Both stubbing and mocking attempt to simulate the behavior of a particular component or layer within an application, without relying on an actual full-featured implementation. This approach helps to focus your testing concerns on the code actually being tested, rather than the details of other layers.

Stubbing usually implies that a particular component is faked, with "canned responses" being returned so that the tested layer is fooled into believing that it is talking to the actual live implementation. Mocking also attempts to simulate a particular layer, but it does more than just return canned responses. A mocked object can also be used to validate expected behavior relating to the layer it is intended to represent. For example, it is possible to specify that a certain method is called on the mock or other details that help provide valuable assertions about how the code you are testing integrates with the mocked layer.

Spring provides several useful mock layers, which can be used as drop-in replacements for various layers within your application. For example, JNDI, Servlet API, and Portlet mock layers that simulate behavior and associated expectations for their respective layers. For mocking other components, it is possible to use frameworks like Mockito, jMock, EasyMock, or MockObjects. These frameworks provide an extensible means for dynamically defining your own mocks.

For our examples, we will use the very powerful Mockito framework. Mockito allows you to define the behavior for a particular class. It also lets you define the expectations for how particular methods on the class are called and what they return within the context of a unit test. Mockito employs a simple DSL that allows you to specify a fairly flexible range of behavior.

Let's look at a unit test that attempts to verify the behavior of the PersonRepository implementation:

```
package com.apress.springpersistence.audiomanager.test;

import org.junit.Assert;
import org.junit.Test;
import org.junit.Before;
import org.junit.runner.RunWith;

import org.mockito.Mock;
import static org.mockito.Mockito.when;
import org.mockito.runners.MockitoJUnitRunner;

import com.apress.springpersistence.audiomanager.domain.Person;
import com.apress.springpersistence.audiomanager.service.PersonRepository;

@RunWith(MockitoJUnitRunner.class)
public class MockitoJUnitTest {

    Person person;

    @Mock
    private PersonRepository personRepository;

    @Before
    public void setUp() {
        person = new Person();
        person.setId((long) 1);
        person.setName("Test User");
        when(personRepository.count()).thenReturn((long) 1);
        when(personRepository.findOne((long) 1)).thenReturn(person);
    }

    @Test
    public void testMockPersonRetrieval() {
        Assert.assertEquals("Test User",
                            personRepository.findOne((long) 1).getName());
    }

    @Test
    public void testThatMockRepositorySaveDoesNothing() {
        Assert.assertEquals(1, this.personRepository.count());
        Person bogusPerson = new Person();
        person.setId((long) 2);
        person.setName("Bogus Test User");
        personRepository.save(bogusPerson);
        Assert.assertNotEquals(2, this.personRepository.count());
    }

}
```

Notice that no external dependencies are required for this unit test—not even Spring. This not only helps to isolate the code that we are testing, but it also significantly speeds up the test.

We declare that we are using the Mockito framework by supplying the `@RunWith(MockitoJUnitRunner.class)` annotation. Next, we declare that the `PersonRepository` should be mocked with the `@Mock` annotation.

In our `setUp` method, we use Mockito's static `when` method to adjust the behavior of the mocked `personRepository`. First, we force the `count` method to always return 1. Then we specify that a call to `findOne` with 123 as the ID should always return the newly created person, Test User.

The two tests here aren't actually good unit tests. They're just meant to demonstrate that the behaviors we put in place are being enforced. In our `testMockPersonRetrieval` test, you'll see that the `personRepository` returns the Test User that we expected. And in `testThatMockRepositorySaveDoesNothing`, calls to save an entity on `personRepository` proceed just fine without throwing an exception, but they don't actually change the state of the object since it's merely a mock and we have no persistence mechanisms configured.

■ **Note**   We encourage you to explore mocking in more detail because it is a powerful tool in the creation of an effective unit-testing strategy. Often, developers focus too much on integration testing, simply because unit testing can seem more complicated when "faking" the behavior of dependencies becomes necessary. Mocking is a pragmatic solution for easily defining the behavior and expectations of dependencies, which encourages the development of more unit tests.

We've presented a cursory overview for unit testing a piece of code in isolation. However, an effective testing strategy also needs to take into consideration how a particular component works within the context of a running application. This is where integration testing comes in, and Spring serves to simplify the development of integration tests by helping to bootstrap your test suite, resolving dependencies, and handling persistence details, such as transactions.

Spring Dependency Injection and Testing

The Spring Framework provides a convenient layer of abstraction called the TestContext Framework, which drastically simplifies switching between testing frameworks. This framework, which was added as a part of Spring 3, helps to abstract away any test framework-specific details. TestContext Framework eliminates the worry about the specifics of a particular testing framework. This makes it especially easy to jump from one testing strategy to another. More importantly, the TestContext Framework simplifies testing details, making it easier to write effective unit and integration tests, to integrate Spring dependencies, and to make useful assertions related to your persistence tier.

Spring testing includes a combination of XML and annotations that affect the way dependencies are injected within a test class. XML configuration works in a similar fashion to the examples you've seen in this book. When defining integration tests, you can use the same XML code (more or less) that you use in your application. However, it is often desirable to override certain beans, such as your datasource, while maintaining the same wiring and implementation details for your application repositories and Service objects. Such a strategy enables you to verify the behavior of your entire persistence tier while leveraging a specialized test database.

There are quite a few Spring-specific annotations available to store the test configuration in your application and the test XML into a running JUnit test. The @RunWith annotation allows you to specify the test framework that you would like to use. As mentioned earlier, one of the primary benefits of using Spring's TestContext Framework is that it allows you to define a test class without tying your code to a particular test framework. You can specify that a particular class is a test by using the @Test annotation. Then, to indicate which test framework should be used to run the test, you can use @RunWith, which allows you to specify the test framework. For the examples in this chapter, we're going to stick with JUnit 4. We place the following annotation at the top of our test class:

```
@RunWith(SpringJUnit4ClassRunner.class)
```

If we want to switch to TestNG, we simply change the value of this annotation. Adding the @RunWith annotation to your unit test class brings Spring into the picture for running the tests and wiring the necessary dependencies. However, there are several options for how the wiring details can be specified. The strategy you choose depends on the unique needs of your application. For instance, if you are building a simple application with only a single datasource, then you can use an autowiring-by-type strategy, which implicitly injects the class that matches the type specified in the setter method on which the annotation is added. However, if your application uses multiple datasources, then an autowiring-by-type approach isn't as trivial. For those scenarios, you should use the @Resource or @Qualifier annotations to disambiguate the dependency that you to want inject.

Although it is usually preferable to let Spring handle dependency injection via configuration or annotation, it's also possible to make your test class implement ApplicationContextAware or to extend AbstractJUnit4SpringContextTests, which gives you direct access to the ApplicationContext, from which you can do a lookup using the bean name:

```
context.getBean("datasource");
```

Now you have a handle on some of the options for injecting the layers on which your test class depends. The question that remains is: How to inject? In our application, we have defined Spring beans in an XML file named spring-master.xml, which imports our spring-persistence.xml configuration. We can import this configuration by adding the following annotation:

```
@ContextConfiguration(locations = {"classpath:/META-INF/spring/spring-master.xml"})
```

The @ContextConfiguration annotation defines the locations of your configuration files. You can determine, on a test-by-test basis, whether to use the Spring configuration file for your full-blown application or to define a more specific unit-testing configuration that is tailored to the needs of a particular test.

Spring configuration via XML is handy, but now you're probably wondering how you can access certain beans that are defined in your configuration or those that were picked up through component scanning. Do you remember the @Autowired annotation that Spring managed beans use? You can use it in your test code to tell the Spring JUnit Runner that you need Spring beans.

As of Spring 4 and the introduction of Spring Boot, a new annotation was added to specify the Spring ApplicationContext you'd like to use for testing. @SpringApplicationConfiguration is similar to the standard ContextConfiguration, but uses the Spring Boot SpringApplicationContextLoader, which allows you to do things like start an embedded servlet container for your tests.

Here's what the PersonRepository test code looks like when we put all of this together:

```
package com.apress.springpersistence.audiomanager.test;

import org.junit.Test;
import org.junit.runner.RunWith;
import org.springframework.beans.factory.annotation.Autowired;
```

```
import org.springframework.boot.test.SpringApplicationConfiguration;
import org.springframework.test.context.junit4.SpringJUnit4ClassRunner;

import com.apress.springpersistence.audiomanager.dao.PersonRepository;
import com.apress.springpersistence.audiomanager.AudioManagerApplication;

@RunWith(SpringJUnit4ClassRunner.class)
@SpringApplicationConfiguration(classes = AudioManagerApplication.class)
public class PersonRepositoryTest {

    @Autowired
    PersonRepository personRepository;

    @Test
    public void testPerson() {
        // insert test logic here
    }

}
```

Let's explore what's happening here. @RunWith tells JUnit that the test needs some extra logic in order to be set up properly. That extra logic comes from an instance of a class that implements JUnit's Runner interface. In our case, we have a Spring Runner called SpringJUnit4ClassRunner that knows how to set up our application context and inject our test with all of the plumbing that it needs using the standard Spring dependency-injection annotations, such as @Autowired. SpringJUnit4ClassRunner also looks for other annotations, including @ContextConfiguration and @Transactional.

As you saw in the example, @SpringApplicationConfiguration(classes = AudioManagerApplication .class) tells SpringJUnit4ClassRunner how to set up your testing environment. The TestContext Framework is responsible for actually performing the @Autowired injection. The TestContext Framework also keeps track of the results of the status of the current test, such as which method and class were run and which exception was thrown as part of the test. @RunWith and @ContextConfiguration are the essential core components of Spring JUnit4 testing.

■ **Note** The TestContext Framework has some performance optimizations to make sure that the framework loads that configuration only once for all tests, if you run multiple test classes that use the same application context configuration. There are quite a few additional advanced features relating to the TestContext Framework that are worth exploring if you need more advanced testing.

Integration Testing with a Database

Now that you know how to write a JUnit test class and configure it with Spring, you're ready to do some database testing! The simplest form of database testing reuses those fancy repositories that you've been working on. You can also apply the usual Spring @Transactional annotations, as well as @TransactionConfiguration, which is an annotation that tells the transactional Spring testing environment whether you would like to commit or roll back the transaction after each test.

The following test takes all of those elements and puts them to work:

```
package com.apress.springpersistence.audiomanager.test;

import org.junit.After;
import org.junit.Assert;
import org.junit.Test;
import org.junit.Before;
import org.junit.runner.RunWith;

import org.springframework.beans.factory.annotation.Autowired;
import org.springframework.boot.test.SpringApplicationConfiguration;
import org.springframework.test.context.junit4.SpringJUnit4ClassRunner;
import org.springframework.test.context.transaction.TransactionConfiguration;
import org.springframework.transaction.annotation.Transactional;

import com.apress.springpersistence.audiomanager.AudioManagerApplication;
import com.apress.springpersistence.audiomanager.domain.Person;
import com.apress.springpersistence.audiomanager.service.PersonRepository;

@Transactional()
@TransactionConfiguration(defaultRollback = true)
@RunWith(SpringJUnit4ClassRunner.class)
@SpringApplicationConfiguration(classes = AudioManagerApplication.class)
public class IntegrationJUnitTest {

    Person person;

    @Autowired
    PersonRepository personRepository;

    @Before
    public void setUp() {
        person = new Person();
        person.setName("Test User");
        personRepository.save(person);
    }

    @After
    public void tearDown() {
        personRepository.delete(person);
        person = null;
    }

    @Test
    public void testPersonPersisted() {
        // recall that our import.sql for this context is
        // inserting 2 users before these tests run
        Assert.assertEquals(3, this.personRepository.count());
    }

}
```

This example is using our web application's Spring context, which means that we're using our in-memory H2 database configuration. With the @Before and @After annotations, we're ensuring that the state of the Person class is correct for each test method invocation. Finally, in nice discrete units, we test the behavior of PersonRepository when making a successful call to findAll() Person entities.

Notice also that we have set defaultRollback = true, which ensures that this method is automatically rolled back after completion. Automatically rolling back your transactions within an integration test is an effective strategy for ensuring that each test method returns the database to its original, pristine state. When defining an integration test that talks to a database, it is important to reduce the potential for database "side effects" and to ensure that each test stands alone, without being affected by or relying upon previously run methods.

Integration Testing for RESTful APIs

We'll discuss the ins and outs of building RESTful APIs in Chapter 10. But in the spirit of TDD, let's lay out the expected behavior that we'd like our system to exhibit, as follows:

```
package com.apress.springpersistence.audiomanager.test;

import org.apache.http.HttpStatus;
import static org.hamcrest.Matchers.*;
import com.jayway.restassured.module.mockmvc.RestAssuredMockMvc;
import static com.jayway.restassured.module.mockmvc.RestAssuredMockMvc.*;

import org.junit.Test;
import org.junit.Before;
import org.junit.runner.RunWith;

import org.springframework.boot.test.WebIntegrationTest;
import org.springframework.web.context.WebApplicationContext;
import org.springframework.beans.factory.annotation.Autowired;
import org.springframework.boot.test.SpringApplicationConfiguration;
import org.springframework.test.context.junit4.SpringJUnit4ClassRunner;

import com.apress.springpersistence.audiomanager.AudioManagerApplication;

@RunWith(SpringJUnit4ClassRunner.class)
@SpringApplicationConfiguration(classes = AudioManagerApplication.class)
@WebIntegrationTest
public class WebIntegrationJUnitTest {

    @Autowired
    private WebApplicationContext context;

    @Before
    public void setUp() {
        RestAssuredMockMvc.webAppContextSetup(context);
    }
```

```
@Test
public void canFetchPlaylist() {
    when().
            get("/playlists/1").
            then().
            statusCode(HttpStatus.SC_OK).
            body("name", is(equalTo("Classic Rock")));
}

}
```

As in the previous example, we're making use of the SpringJUnit4ClassRunner.class in the @RunWith annotation. And again, we're leveraging the convenience of @SpringApplicationConfiguration for testing in a Spring Boot application. What's new, however, is the @WebIntegrationTest annotation. This annotation lets the context loader know that we need a web application to execute the tests contained in this class. This allows you to take advantage of TestRestTemplate, which is a convenience subclass of RestTemplate that's specifically intended for integration tests for RESTful APIs. In our example, however, we've elected to use a very convenient little library called REST Assured.

To add REST Assured to our project, you need to add a new dependency to pom.xml. As with the spring-boot-starter-test dependency we added in the beginning of the chapter, we're restricting REST Assured to the Maven test life cycles by specifying the test scope.

```
<dependency>
    <groupId>com.jayway.restassured</groupId>
    <artifactId>spring-mock-mvc</artifactId>
    <version>2.4.1</version>
    <scope>test</scope>
</dependency>
```

The REST Assured library provides a convenient Java DSL on top of Groovy's HTTPBuilder, which in turn builds on top of Apache HTTPClient. In our opinion, this DSL makes reading these tests incredibly simple and provides enormous power. REST Assured supports the POST, GET, PUT, DELETE, OPTIONS, PATCH, and HEAD HTTP methods. It also easily provides mechanisms to specify and verify values for parameters, headers, cookies and the response body. Further, you can take advantage of XPath, XmlPath, or JsonPath to inspect the body of an HTTPResponse to test for the results you expect.

First, we have to initialize REST Assured with Spring WebApplicationContext in the setUp method. Then, using REST Assured's static when() method, we can succinctly express that we want to issue an HTTP GET for the resource "/playlists/1" and then() we expect HTTP 200 status code to be returned with the name of the playlist that we specified in our import.sql configuration.

The body() portion of the test is where we see the Hamcrest matchers coming into play. The is() matcher is nothing more than syntactic sugar for improving readability. The equalTo() matcher tests object equality by using Object.equals.

We hope that this example piqued your interest in both REST Assured and Hamcrest. We've found them to be very beneficial in writing tests that strike the right balance in specificity so that your tests aren't so brittle that they must constantly be revised, or so lax that they fail to catch bugs as they're introduced to a code base.

Summary

This chapter introduced strategies for testing Spring applications using unit and integration tests. Despite being a well-known best practice, writing tests remains something that far too many developers treat as optional or burdensome because they appear to represent additional up-front costs in terms of time. Once you get into the habit of writing tests, you'll begin to notice that you're spending a lot less time chasing down bugs. You'll notice that thinking about how you test your code leads you to naturally create more flexible, extensible, and decoupled applications.

Of course, you can do a lot more testing with both JUnit and Spring than we were able to cover in this chapter. Not to mention the really powerful testing constructs made possible by the mocking frameworks like Mockito, and DSLs like REST Assured. The documentation for these projects tends to be quite good, and you'll find large communities on sites like StackOverflow.com, which is more than happy to help you learn how to best take advantage of these techniques should you have questions.

And while it's beyond the scope of this book, we would definitely advocate that you investigate performance testing and load testing, which are extremely relevant to applications that entail persistence.

■ ■ ■

CHAPTER 8

Best Practices and Advanced Techniques

Throughout this book, you've learned a lot about the workings of the Spring and Hibernate frameworks. In this chapter, you will learn the techniques necessary for building a performant, production-ready application. Although Hibernate and Spring are relatively easy to bootstrap, their default settings are appropriate only for simple applications. If you are building an application with significant load or performance requirements, you will likely need to do some fine-tuning in order to attain peak performance. In most scenarios, you can circumvent performance issues simply by leveraging the appropriate optimization or architectural strategies.

Lazy Loading Issues

Lazy loading has long been regarded as one of Hibernate's most valuable features, especially with respect to improving performance. By declaring a domain object's association or property to be lazy, an application can avoid undue overhead on the underlying database, which can often lead to faster response times and smaller datasets—both favorable qualities.

Without lazy loading, a simple query may be unnecessarily executed over and over again, or worse yet, a query for a single domain entity might force the loading of an entire object graph, as Hibernate attempts to traverse from one association to the next.

The problem is that lazy loading is a double-edged sword. It is vital for maintaining decent loading performance, but is also a significant risk for major performance problems. While lazy loading reduces the amount of data (as well as the potential for table joins) loaded from the database, this laziness can be very problematic for data that might need to be loaded from the database anyway.

This is not to imply that lazy loading is a bad feature or that it should be disabled. It is a misunderstood problem that is very dependent on the context.

Let's begin by looking at one of the most common and significant issues related to lazy loading that affects persistence-based applications.

© Paul Fisher and Brian D. Murphy 2016
P. Fisher and B.D. Murphy, *Spring Persistence with Hibernate*, DOI 10.1007/978-1-4842-0268-5_8

The N+1 Selects Problem

Let's examine the way in which lazy loading works in a typical use case. In our sample application, our `CreativeWork` domain object contains a one-to-many association to the `Comment` domain object. In other words, a `CreativeWork` contains a collection of `Comment` instances:

```
@Entity
@PrimaryKeyJoinColumn(name="THING_URL")
public class CreativeWork extends Thing {

    @ManyToOne
    private Thing about;
    private String accessibilityAPI;
    private String accessibilityControl;
    private String accessibilityFeature;
    private String accessibilityHazard;
    @ManyToOne
    private Person accountablePerson;
    @ManyToOne
    private AggregateRating aggregateRating;
    private String alternativeHeadline;
    @ManyToOne
    private MediaObject associatedMedia;
    @ManyToOne
    private AudioObject audio;
    @ManyToOne
    private Person author;
    private String award;
    private String citiation;
    @OneToMany
    private List<Comment> comments;
    private Integer commentCount;

    . . .

    public List<Comment> getComments() {
      return comments;
    }

    public void setComments(List<Comment> comments) {
      this.comments = comments;
    }

    . . .

}
```

By default, the `java.util.List` of Comment entities is declared lazy. Let's consider what happens under the hood when we attempt to load all the `comments` for a series of `CreativeWork` entities.

```
entityManager.createQuery("SELECT cw FROM CreativeWork cw").getResultList();
```

Assuming there is at least one row in the `CreativeWork` table, the preceding statements will return a list of `CreativeWork` instances. However, because our `comments` association (within the `CreativeWork` class) is declared lazy, Hibernate will not perform a SQL join in an attempt to load data from both the `CreativeWork` table and the related rows from the `Comment` table. Instead of loading these `Comment` rows from the database, Hibernate populates the `comments` property for each of the returned `CreativeWork` instances with a proxy object.

For collections, Hibernate provides persistent collection implementations that serve as *proxies* for the collection associations in our domain model. For instance, our `comments` property is declared as a `java.util.List`. Hibernate sets this property to an instance of `org.hibernate.collection.PersistentList`, a special class designed to intercept attempts to access the referenced collection so that a lazy collection can be initialized.

Hibernate generates proxies for each domain object within an application and uses these proxies for single-ended associations that are marked as lazy. For example, we can define the inverse side of the `CreativeWork->Comment` many-to-one association—which is represented by the `creativeWork` property within the `Comment` domain object—as lazy by using the `fetch` parameter to the `@ManyToOne` annotation:

```
@Entity
@PrimaryKeyJoinColumn(name="THING_URL")
public class Comment extends CreativeWork {

    @ManyToOne(fetch=FetchType.LAZY)
    private CreativeWork creativeWork;

    private Integer downvoteCount;
    private Integer upvoteCount;

    public CreativeWork getCreativeWork() {
        return creativeWork;
    }

    public void setCreativeWork(CreativeWork creativeWork) {
        this.creativeWork = creativeWork;
    }

}
```

This snippet prevents a `Comment`'s reference to the associated `CreativeWork` from being loaded from the database — until the property is accessed (which triggers the proxy to make a call to the database).

The goal of these proxies is to serve as placeholders of sorts. For data that is not loaded from the database, Hibernate can't simply ignore these properties. Instead, a proxy can be used to defer loading behavior. If no attempt is made to access an uninitialized, lazy property, then nothing will happen. However, if an attempt is made to access one of these proxies, then the proxy will intercept this request and trigger a callback into the database. The end result is that the lazy property is initialized with the relevant data from the database.

All of this sounds pretty ideal. But let's consider what happens if we want to iterate through multiple Comment instances across numerous CreativeWork instances. When a given `CreativeWork` instance is first loaded, the `comments` association is set to an instance of `org.hibernate.collection.PersistentList`. Now imagine that we want to iterate through all the `comments` for all of the `CreativeWork` instances returned in our original query.

```
for (CreativeWork creativeWork: creativeWorks) {
    for (Comment comment: creativeWork.getComments()) {
        // implicitly initialize another collection here
        System.out.println("art:" + comment.getTitle());
    }
}
```

Although this code may seem innocuous, there is actually a serious performance issue hiding between the lines. Since the comments association is not yet initialized when we first retrieve each CreativeWork instance, we are actually initializing each comments association within each successive iteration of the loop. Because Hibernate has no way to infer what we are trying to do, it simply initializes each instance as we reference it. The result is a separate SQL query for each item within the collection. So for the preceding loop, we are actually inadvertently making (*number of categories*) + 1 queries! Suddenly, lazy loading doesn't seem like such an optimization technique anymore.

This disturbingly common scenario is known as the *N+1 selects* issue, in that a select query is issued *N* times (one for each item returned by the original query), plus the original query to load the entity containing the collection in the first place.

A similar predicament occurs for other associations, such as in the many-to-one reference to the CreativeWork domain object from the Comment class. In this scenario, if a list of Comment instances were to be loaded, an additional select query would be initiated each time an attempt was made to access the creativeWork property. Suppose a template within the view layer iterated through a long list of comments in an attempt to display related information about the comment and its associated CreativeWork. This has the potential of requiring hundreds of additional round-trips to the database!

Understanding the potential for this problem is the first step, but how do we go about preventing the N+1 selects issue? Unfortunately, there is no single solution. (If there were, it would probably be an implicit part of Hibernate or JPA.) Each situation may require a slightly different approach. Fortunately, several strategies can help mitigate this potentially damaging scenario. The goal, of course, is to limit the number of SQL queries and attempt to load all the necessary data as efficiently as possible.

Less Lazy Mappings

One solution to the N+1 selects problem is to update your mapping configuration for the affected domain classes. The default behavior for collections is to be lazy and to initialize the collection via a SQL SELECT when the association is accessed. This default strategy is known as *select fetching*, as a second SELECT is issued in order to initialize the lazy association or property. The simplest solution is to override this default behavior, preventing the property from being lazy in the first place.

Let's refactor the mapping configuration affecting the comments association on our CreativeWork instance, as follows:

```
@OneToMany
@Fetch(FetchMode.JOIN)
public List<Comment> getComments() {
    return this.comments;
}
```

By adding the @Fetch annotation, specifying a FetchMode of JOIN, we request that Hibernate automatically initialize our comments collection by using a left outer join when a particular CreativeWork instance is loaded. Hibernate is affected by this @Fetch directive when navigating to a particular CreativeWork instance, loading an instance via get() or load(), or when loading CreativeWork instances via the Criteria API. Alternatively, you can opt to specify FetchMode.SUBSELECT, which will instead load the comments collection by including a SQL subselect as part of the initial query. In either case, the end result is that the comments association is no longer lazy, and an additional query is not required to initialize each comments association.

So problem solved, right? Not exactly. Remember how we mentioned that lazy loading is actually a pretty important feature, and that without it, you risk inadvertently loading too much of your entire database into memory? In other words, you may not always need the comments association, and in those circumstances, you are better off keeping the property as lazy.

So, sometimes it's good to be lazy, like on weekends and on vacation when you're catching up on rest. But other times being lazy can get you into trouble (especially at work). Hibernate is the same way. The best way of solving the N+1 selects problem is to keep your associations declared lazy by default, but override this behavior when you know the association is needed. For example, using JPQL, we could write the following query:

```
List creativeWorks = entityManager.createQuery("SELECT creativeWorks FROM
CreativeWork creativeWorks

LEFT JOIN FETCH creativeWorks.comments

WHERE creativeWorks.id = :id").getResultList();
```

As part of this JPQL query. we issue a LEFT JOIN FETCH. This forces Hibernate to initialize our comments association, overriding the default lazy behavior in the mapping file.

One problem with the approach described earlier is that you end up needing multiple DAO methods to define different loading strategies. For instance, you may end up with the following as one DAO method within the CreativeWorkDao interface:

```
List<CreativeWork> findAllCreativeWorksByAuthor(Author author);
```

And then another DAO method defined as follows:

```
List<CreativeWork>findAllCreativeWorksByAuthorWithComments(Author author);
```

While this approach works, you can imagine how things might become rather complex when a class within your domain model contains multiple associations. Do you need a different DAO method for every possible permutation of the association fetch strategy?

To simplify this situation, JPA 2.1 introduced a concept called NamedEntityGraph, which allows you to include multiple annotations within your domain model that define different loading strategies in terms of which associations should be eagerly fetched. You can reference these loading strategies within your DAO method without having to define multiple methods to represent each approach. The following illustrates this concept further:

```
@Entity
@PrimaryKeyJoinColumn(name="THING_URL")
@NamedEntityGraphs({
    @NamedEntityGraph(
        name = "creativeWorkWithComments",
        attributeNodes = {
            @NamedAttributeNode("comments")
        }
    ),
```

```
@NamedEntityGraph(
    name = "creativeWorkWithCommentsAndAudio",
    attributeNodes = {
        @NamedAttributeNode(value = "comments", subgraph = "audioGraph")
    },
    subgraphs = {
        @NamedSubgraph(
            name = "audioGraph",
            attributeNodes = {
                @NamedAttributeNode("audio")
            }
        )
    }
)
})
public class CreativeWork extends Thing {

    @ManyToOne
    private Thing about;
    private String accessibilityAPI;
    private String accessibilityControl;
    private String accessibilityFeature;
    private String accessibilityHazard;
    @ManyToOne
    private Person accountablePerson;
    @ManyToOne
    private AggregateRating aggregateRating;
    private String alternativeHeadline;
    @ManyToOne
    private MediaObject associatedMedia;
    @ManyToOne
    private AudioObject audio;
    @ManyToOne
    private Person author;
    private String award;
    private String citiation;
    @OneToMany
    private List<Comment> comments;
```

With the NamedEntityGraphs defined, we can specify the associations and subgraphs to fetch from the database simply by stating the appropriate entityGraph from within a DAO method:

```
public interface CreativeWorkRepository extends PagingAndSortingRepository<Thing, URL> {

    @EntityGraph("creativeWorkWithComments")
    List<CreativeWork> findByAuthor(Person author);

    @EntityGraph("creativeWorkWithCommentsAndAudio")
    List<CreativeWork> findByAuthorWithAudio(Person author);

}
```

Batching for Performance

Another strategy for reducing the number of SQL queries required to load data is to use Hibernate's batching feature, which loads multiple entities or collections. Batching offers a slightly simpler solution than controlling lazy loading. You attempt to grab data in batches to prevent this data from being loaded in many more "single queries" later on. The advantage of batching is that it can help improve performance without requiring significant changes to queries or code.

The @BatchSize annotation can be added to a domain entity or to a particular association. Let's update our comments association in our CreativeWork class again to see how we might be able to use Hibernate's batching feature:

```
@ManyToMany
@BatchSize(size = 10)
public List<Comment> getComments() {
    return this.comments;
}
```

Now, even though our comments association is still lazy by default, Hibernate gets ahead of us and attempts to initialize more than just a single comments collection at a time. It accomplishes this by using a SQL in condition, passing in ten identifiers of a CreativeWork instance when loading from the Comment table.

In other words, batching works similarly to the default lazy configuration. First, a CreativeWork is loaded, and then its comments association is loaded in a separate query (when the comments property is accessed, of course). However, with batching enabled, Hibernate attempts to load more than one comments association, querying for the number of associations specified in the size attribute of the @BatchSize annotation.

Keep in mind that @BatchSize doesn't attempt to load multiple items within a collection. A collection is normally initialized in entirety via a separate select. Rather, @BatchSize loads multiple associations to preclude initialization of other associations in our other CreativeWork instances (using our example).

Lazy Initialization Exceptions

Another common issue is the ominous LazyInitializationException. You can probably infer what this exception means by its name: Hibernate is unable to initialize a lazy property. What circumstances account for such a problem?

As we discussed in Chapter 4, a domain object's persistent state is managed through Hibernate's implementation of the EntityManager interface. If a new domain object is instantiated, it is considered transient until it becomes associated with the EntityManager. Similarly, an already persistent domain object can continue to be persistent if the EntityManager is closed, which transitions the entity to a detached state. However, changes to this domain object will not be "recorded" until the domain object transitions back to a Managed state by being reassociated with another EntityManager.

A domain object that has become disassociated from an EntityManager is called a *detached object*. Hibernate is able to detect changes made to a detached domain object and propagate these changes to the database once the instance is reassociated. However, there are some things that are difficult to work around when an EntityManager is closed, and lazy properties are one of those things.

As you learned in the previous section, Hibernate implements laziness by referencing uninitialized properties with proxies—either special persistent collection implementations or proxy classes, depending on the type of association or property. These proxies are able to defer the loading of an association until an attempt is made to access them. Once that happens, the proxies will access the EntityManager and attempt to load the necessary data from the database. Obviously, this can't happen if the EntityManager is closed, so a LazyInitializationException is thrown.

147

The most common cause of a `LazyInitializationException` stems from failing to initialize a collection or lazy property in a DAO or controller method, instead leaving a template within the view layer to discover an uninitialized property. The problem is that Hibernate will close the `EntityManager` by default whenever a persistent operation completes. In the case of a DAO or service method, the `EntityManager` is normally closed when these relevant methods return.

The best way to prevent the `LazyInitializationException` is to ensure that all lazy associations and properties that are required by the view are successfully initialized before the domain objects are passed to the view layer. Fortunately, Spring provides some solutions that help to prevent the occurrence of `LazyInitializationExceptions`, even when lazy properties are not properly initialized before passing domain objects to the view. There are a couple of variations on the solution, but they both employ the same general strategy: defer the closing of the `EntityManager` until after the view has finished rendering.

Now Open Late: Keeping EntityManager Open Past Its Bedtime

Deferring the `EntityManager` from being closed is now typically known as the Open EntityManager In View pattern. The simplest approach for applying this strategy is to use a servlet filter, as described in the next section. However, if you are using Spring MVC, an alternative is to use an interceptor.

The interceptor technique essentially opens an `EntityManager` at the beginning of a servlet request and binds the `EntityManager` to the current thread, allowing it to be accessed by Spring's Hibernate support classes. Then, at the end of the request, the `EntityManager` is closed and unbound from the thread. This is a bit of an oversimplification, and the implementation details differ slightly, depending on whether you are using the servlet filter or the controller interceptor. However, the basic concepts are the same: open an `EntityManager` and associate it with the active thread to be used by persistence-related methods, and then ensure the `EntityManager` is kept open until the request completes. Because the request doesn't complete until after the view rendering has finished processing, the potential for the `LazyInitializationException` is significantly reduced.

Using the Open EntityManager In View pattern is relatively simple. If you are already using Spring MVC, you can define the `OpenEntityManagerInViewInterceptor` class as a new bean, adding it to your Spring MVC configuration, like so:

```
<bean name="openEntityManagerInViewInterceptor"
    class="org.springframework.orm.jpa.support
                        .OpenEntityManagerInViewInterceptor" />
```

With your `OpenEntityManagerInViewInterceptor` defined, you then need to add this interceptor to your list of MVC interceptors. The interceptors defined in this list are invoked (in order) as part of the request-processing flow of each MVC controller. Spring MVC controllers provide hooks into the life cycle of an MVC controller, such as `preHandle`, `postHandle`, and `afterCompletion`. Spring 4 provides an easy way to globally define interceptors. Let's take a look at an MVC configuration file.

```
<?xml version="1.0" encoding="UTF-8" standalone="no"?>
<beans xmlns="http://www.springframework.org/schema/beans"
        xmlns:aop="http://www.springframework.org/schema/aop"
        xmlns:context="http://www.springframework.org/schema/context"
        xmlns:jee="http://www.springframework.org/schema/jee"
        xmlns:tx="http://www.springframework.org/schema/tx"
        xmlns:xsi="http://www.w3.org/2001/XMLSchema-instance"
        xmlns:repository="http://www.springframework.org/schema/data/repository"
        xmlns:mvc="http://www.springframework.org/schema/mvc"
```

```
    xsi:schemaLocation="http://www.springframework.org/schema/jee
      http://www.springframework.org/schema/jee/spring-jee-4.1.xsd
      http://www.springframework.org/schema/aop
      http://www.springframework.org/schema/aop/spring-aop-4.1.xsd
      http://www.springframework.org/schema/data/repository
      http://www.springframework.org/schema/data/repository/spring-repository-1.6.xsd
      http://www.springframework.org/schema/beans
      http://www.springframework.org/schema/beans/spring-beans-4.1.xsd
      http://www.springframework.org/schema/tx
      http://www.springframework.org/schema/tx/spring-tx-4.1.xsd
      http://www.springframework.org/schema/context
      http://www.springframework.org/schema/context/spring-context-4.1.xsd
      http://www.springframework.org/schema/mvc
      http://www.springframework.org/schema/mvc/spring-mvc.xsd">


<context:spring-configured />


<mvc:interceptors>
    <bean class="org.springframework.orm.jpa.support
                            .OpenEntityManagerInViewInterceptor" />
</mvc:interceptors>


<context:component-scan base-package="com.apress.springpersistence">
    <context:exclude-filter
        expression="org.springframework.stereotype.Controller"
        type="annotation" />
</context:component-scan>


<bean id="jsonView"
      class="org.springframework.web.servlet.view.json
                                    .MappingJackson2JsonView" />

</beans>
```

In this example, we use the `mvc:annotation-driven` and `component-scan` features to allow us to enable those Spring life-cycle features and to define our controllers via annotation (meaning we can add `@Controller` to the class and Spring will integrate these classes as controllers, provided they are in the appropriate package path). Also notice that we added our `OpenEntityManagerInViewInterceptor` inline within the `mvc:interceptors` block. Any interceptor beans defined here will have the appropriate methods invoked within the various stages of the request life cycle.

Applying the OpenEntityManager Filter

If you aren't using Spring MVC, or just don't want to use an interceptor approach, you can instead add the `OpenEntityManagerInViewFilter` to your `web.xml` file. The approach is roughly the same as the interceptor technique, except the hooks for opening and closing the `EntityManager` occur at the servlet-request level rather than at the controller level.

Here is how you might add the `OpenEntityManagerInViewFilter` to your application's `web.xml` file:

```xml
<!-- binds a JPA EntityManager to the thread for the entire processing of the request -->
<filter>
    <filter-name>OpenEntityManagerInViewFilter</filter-name>
    <filter-class>
        org.springframework.orm.jpa.support.OpenEntityManagerInViewFilter
    </filter-class>
</filter>

<!--Map the EntityManager Filter to all requests -->
<filter-mapping>
    <filter-name>OpenEntityManagerInViewFilter</filter-name>
    <url-pattern>/*</url-pattern>
</filter-mapping>
```

This snippet is an excerpt from a `web.xml` file that references the filter definition and mapping necessary for integrating the `OpenEntityManagerInViewFilter`. It is important that you set the appropriate `filter-mapping` glob pattern, because this defines to which URLs processing should be applied.

Caching

So far, we have discussed a few strategies for reducing or optimizing trips to the database. Even better than improving the ways in which data is queried is to preclude the need for accessing the database at all. Obviously, some database access is always needed, but caching can go quite a long way toward minimizing database load and improving application performance.

One of Hibernate's greatest advantages is that it gives developers many features "for free." And one of these free features is implicit caching. If you were to decide to implement a persistence layer using plain JDBC, you would need to explicitly integrate caching within your DAO methods or at some lower level of abstraction. While caching may seem trivial to implement on the surface, you will begin to perceive the complexity when you consider the rules for invalidation (the factors that cause a particular item in the cache to be expired), preventing conflicts, and handling a cached item's time to live (TTL).

So if Hibernate provides all of these caching features for free, what is the benefit of understanding the mechanics of caching? Although Hibernate includes some foundational caching features that provide basic optimizations to limit any unnecessary trips to the database, tuning its default caching behavior can significantly improve your application's performance.

To leverage caching for improved application performance, you need to understand the different layers of caching within Hibernate and what can actually be cached. For all domain objects, Hibernate provides two distinct caching levels:

- The first-level, or L1, cache is provided by the `EntityManager`, and therefore relates only to the limited scope of a particular user or request. The first-level cache is designed primarily as an optimization, preventing the requerying of domain objects that have already been loaded.

- The second-level, or L2, cache is scoped to the `EntityManagerFactory`, and therefore is longer-lived and can provide caching capabilities across multiple users and requests. The second-level cache provides the most utility and flexibility for optimization through caching.

So, the approach is to activate the second-level cache and integrate a cache provider to start caching. Now we need to consider what can be cached.

Hibernate caches domain objects in slightly different ways. Each top-level domain object is cached within a different region. A *region* is essentially a different section or namespace, intended to partition each entity and prevent the potential for clashes. Each domain object is persisted to a cache using its identifier as the key. So, given a cache region and an identifier, you are able to access the data for a particular domain object. Each domain object is cached by storing the values of its respective properties.

However, a domain object's references and collections are persisted *separately* from a domain object. In other words, the cached representation of a domain object will reference only the identifiers of its references. For example, many-to-one associations are persisted as a single ID, while a collection is persisted as a list of identifiers. Domain object collections are actually persisted within a separate cache region, intended specifically for that particular collection. The key in this case is still the parent domain object's identifier, but the region is specific to the domain object and the collection name. The value, however, is a list of identifiers, where each identifier in the list corresponds to the ID of each entity referenced in the original collection.

Hibernate uses this strategy because it is more efficient to just store the IDs of each entity within a collection, rather than the data of every entity in its entirety. The intention is that having the IDs should be enough, since the full data should be cached elsewhere, within the referenced domain object's own cache region. Furthermore, caching references as identifiers decouples the domain objects to which they relate, ensuring that changes to the referenced domain objects are cached only in a single location. This is obviously far simpler than managing a complex dependency tree—especially when you begin to consider the complexity of invalidating a particular item when it expires or when an update is made to the database.

Integrating a Caching Implementation

Hibernate provides a generic abstraction layer for caching functionality, allowing numerous caching implementations to be easily plugged in to the Hibernate infrastructure. There are a variety of excellent caching solutions, including Ehcache, JBoss Infinispan, and many more. Each caching implementation differs slightly in the feature set it provides. For instance, some implementations offer clustering capability, allowing multiple nodes within a cluster to share the same caching data (which can reduce the potential for cache conflicts and stale data). Some caching solutions provide specialized features, such as transactional behavior.

■ **Note**　The choice of which cache provider to use depends on your requirements. Generally, we recommend Ehcache, a flexible open source caching implementation that provides clustering capability. If your application has requirements for a transactional cache or other specific needs, you should take a look at some of the other cache provider choices.

Let's revisit our `persistence.xml` configuration and modify it to incorporate Ehcache.

```xml
<?xml version="1.0" encoding="UTF-8" standalone="no"?>
<persistence xmlns="http://java.sun.com/xml/ns/persistence"
             xmlns:xsi="http://www.w3.org/2001/XMLSchema-instance" version="2.0"
             xsi:schemaLocation="http://java.sun.com/xml/ns/persistence
             http://java.sun.com/xml/ns/persistence/persistence_2_0.xsd">

    <persistence-unit name="persistenceUnit"
                      transaction-type="RESOURCE_LOCAL">

        <provider>org.hibernate.jpa.HibernatePersistenceProvider</provider>
        <mapping-file>META-INF/orm.xml</mapping-file>
        <shared-cache-mode>ENABLE_SELECTIVE</shared-cache-mode>
```

```
        <properties>
            <property name="hibernate.dialect"
                    value="org.hibernate.dialect.H2Dialect" />
            <!--
                value='create' to build a new database on each run;
                value='update' to modify an existing database;
                value='create-drop' to create and drop tables on each run;
                value='validate' makes no changes to the database
              -->
            <property name="hibernate.hbm2ddl.auto" value="create" />
            <property name="hibernate.show_sql" value="true" />
            <property name="hibernate.cache.use_second_level_cache"
                    value="true" />
            <property name="hibernate.cache.provider_class"
                    value="net.sf.ehcache.hibernate.SingletonEhCacheProvider"/>
            <property name="hibernate.ejb.naming_strategy"
                    value="org.hibernate.cfg.ImprovedNamingStrategy"/>
        </properties>

    </persistence-unit>

</persistence>
```

Here, we enable second-level caching by setting the hibernate.cache.use_second_level_cache property on the persistence unit to true. Then we specify the cache implementation, ehcache, via the hibernate.cache.provider_class property.

Once you've activated the second-level cache and selected a cache provider, you have officially started caching. Next, you need to configure the caching rules.

Determining Caching Rules

To configure the caching rules for your domain model, the simplest approach is to add the @Cache annotation to your domain objects. As an example, let's examine the caching configuration of the CreativeWork domain object in our art gallery application:

```
@Entity
@Cacheable
public class CreativeWork implements DomainObject {

    private Long id;
    . . .
    private List<Comment> comments = new ArrayList<Comment>();

    @Id
    @GeneratedValue
    public final Long getId() {
        return id;
    }
    public void setId(Long id) {
        this.id = id;
    }
```

```
. . .

@OneToMany
@Cache(usage=CacheConcurrencyStrategy.READ_WRITE)
public List<Comment> getComments() {
    return this.comments;
}


. . .

}
```

Here, we have added a @Cache annotation in two places: at the top of the entity, which serves as the configuration for caching the domain object itself, and above our one-to-many comments association. Therefore, we have defined the caching rules for both the CreativeWork domain object itself and the CreativeWork domain object's comments collection.

In the first instance of the @Cache annotation, we also set the region attribute. This allows us to set the region within which we persist our cached data. We omitted this attribute for the comments collection, which will then allow Hibernate to use the default region setting. The region default is the class name (including the package). For collections, the region default is the full class name, followed by .<collectionname>. So in the case of the comments collection, the default region name is com.apress.springpersistence.audiomanager.core.domain.CreativeWork.comments. Of course, we could choose to override this instead by specifying a region for the collection.

The @Cache annotation's usage attribute defines the cache strategy to use for the configured entity or collection. When using Ehcache, there are three options:

- The read-only setting should be used only when the data to be cached will never be updated. A read-only cache strategy provides the best performance, since cached data will never need to expire or be invalidated.

- The nonstrict-read-write setting should be used when concurrent access of data is unlikely, as the caching implementation will not attempt to lock the cache to prevent contention or version mismatch.

- The read-write setting is suitable when concurrent access and updating of data is likely, because this approach provides the semantics of a read-committed isolation level.

Configuring Cache Regions

Next, you need to set up the configuration for the regions into which your data will be persisted. Ehcache employs an XML configuration file that is loaded at application startup. Typically, the file is called ehcache.xml and placed at the root of the classpath. However, you can override this default location by setting the following properties in your persistence.xml file:

```
<prop key="hibernate.cache.region.factory_class">
    net.sf.ehcache.hibernate.EhCacheRegionFactory
</prop>
<prop key="net.sf.ehcache.configurationResourceName">
    /path/to/ehcache.xml
</prop>
```

The default ehcache.xml file that ships with Ehcache includes a default cache configuration that contains the settings used for any region that is not explicitly defined. However, it is usually a good idea to configure each cache region you plan to include in your application. Here is an example of the definition of our cache regions for our CreativeWork domain object and the CreativeWork.comments collection:

```
<cache name="CreativeWork"
       maxElementsInMemory="10000"
       eternal="false"
       timeToIdleSeconds="300"
       timeToLiveSeconds="600"
       overflowToDisk="true"
/>

<cache name=" com.apress.springpersistence.audiomanager.core.domain.CreativeWork.comments"
       maxElementsInMemory="10000"
       eternal="false"
       timeToIdleSeconds="300"
       timeToLiveSeconds="600"
       overflowToDisk="false"
/>
```

We have defined two cache regions, as specified by the name attribute. Typically, the name attribute for a domain object includes the fully qualified class name (including package). However, in our earlier caching configuration of the CreativeWork domain object (the listing in the previous section), we explicitly changed the default region attribute, using the shorter region name CreativeWork instead. We left the default region value for the comments collection.

These cache region settings work as follows:

- maxElementsInMemory specifies the maximum number of cached entities to store in this region. We used a value of 10000 for both cache regions, but it is important to consider this number very carefully. Using too high of a value can cause OutOfMemoryException issues, as well as degrade performance. Because object sizes and access patterns can vary so much from application to application, it is a good idea to experiment with these settings and profile your application to determine optimal values.

- eternal specifies whether a cache region should "live forever." This value can come in handy (along with overFlowToDisk) when you want to keep your cache prepopulated in between restarts. This is also valuable in situations when it might take a lot of time to populate your cache. A value of true for eternal will ensure that your cached data will persist, even when the application needs to be restarted.

- timeToIdleSeconds specifies how long a cached item will stay in the cache when there are no attempts to access it. For instance, if a particular CreativeWork instance is stored in the cache but there are no attempts to load this value from the cache for a while, then the benefit of keeping this item cached is questionable. It is a good idea to keep this setting to around half of the timeToLiveSeconds attribute value.

- timeToLiveSeconds corresponds to an entity's TTL—the amount of time before the cached entity expires and the data is purged from the cache, regardless of last access.

- `overFlowToDisk` specifies that if the `maxElementsInMemory` is exceeded, Ehcache should begin storing overflow on disk. While this setting sounds useful, keep in mind that persisting data on disk incurs significant performance penalties when compared to memory storage. You are using caching because you have a database for persisting data permanently. Of course, data cached on disk will outperform a database, but you should still consider this setting carefully.

It is very important to carefully consider your TTL values. Setting these values too high increases the potential for stale data and version conflicts. This risk is significantly increased in situations where an application is deployed in a clustered configuration (but the cache for each application server node is not shared). In a typical cluster configuration, updates made to one node will invalidate that node's cache, but these changes won't propagate to the caches of other nodes in the cluster. One solution is to use a lower TTL value for the `timeToLiveSeconds` attribute, which reduces the likelihood of stale data in the cache. A better solution is to use a clusterable caching solution, which allows all the nodes in the cluster to use a shared cache, significantly reducing the potential for conflicts and stale data. We will discuss clustered caching strategies later in this chapter.

Caching Your Queries

Much like collections caching, query caching attempts to store only the identifiers of the entities returned by a particular query's result. By default, queries are all cached within a single region, but you can override this setting by specifying a region name for a particular query, forcing the query to be cached elsewhere. The key for a particular cached query is composed of the query along with the identifiers or values of each of the query's parameters. This approach ensures that the results of each cached query are cached separately. If the same query is invoked with slightly different parameters, the cache will not be used.

While caching of your domain objects and collections is more a part of the default configuration, query caching requires a few additional steps. First, the second-level cache must be enabled, as described in the previous section. Next, the following property must be set to true in your `persistence.xml` file:

```
<property name="hibernate.cache.use_query_cache" value="true"/>
```

Hibernate leverages an additional cache region for powering its query cache implementation: the `UpdateTimestampsCache`. This cache region should also be configured explicitly in the Ehcache configuration file. Here is a sample configuration:

```
<cache name="org.hibernate.cache.UpdateTimestampsCache"
       maxElementsInMemory="5000"
       eternal="true"
       overflowToDisk="true"/>
```

Here, we specified that this cache region should be `eternal`. This is the recommended setting for the `UpdateTimestampsCache`, but at the very least, the TTL should be longer than the TTL of any of the query cache regions.

If you decide to use the default cache region for all query caches, you could configure the following in Ehcache for your query cache:

```
<cache name="org.hibernate.cache.StandardQueryCache"
       maxElementsInMemory="500"
       eternal="false"
       timeToLiveSeconds="120"
       overflowToDisk="true"/>
```

This configuration defines the cache region settings for the queries to be cached.

```
┌──────────────────────────────────────────────────────────────────────────┐
│                        A QUERY CACHING CAVEAT                              │
└──────────────────────────────────────────────────────────────────────────┘
```

We strongly recommend doing some performance testing before attempting to use query caching, as it can actually degrade performance rather than improve it.

The reason query caching can sometimes cause worse performance than not using it at all is due to the use of the `UpdateTimestampsCache`. This region keeps track of the most recent updates for all tables within the application, storing timestamps for each table corresponding to the last time that a particular table was updated. When a query is invoked, even if the result data is still stored in the cache, if Hibernate detects that a table associated with your query has changed since your query was cached, it will invalidate the query data, and you must hit the database instead of the cache. Therefore, if your application incurs frequent updates across any of your tables, the benefits of query caching become reduced. Furthermore, because any update to any table also means changes to the `UpdateTimestampsCache`, this resource becomes a potential for bottlenecks, due to lock contention. Suddenly, query caching doesn't sound so useful.

We don't want to discourage you, however. It is important to understand the way in which the query caching feature works, so that you can better evaluate your requirements and determine whether it is appropriate for your application.

Caching in a Clustered Configuration

If you are building an application that is intended to handle a high volume of requests, you will likely need to set up multiple application nodes in a clustered configuration. Although having multiple nodes will provide more resources for your application, if each node maintains its own cache, you will begin to strain the database. With each additional node added to the cluster, you will increase database load commensurately, such that the number of nodes in your cluster will represent the factor of database request volume:

$$(Num\ Nodes\ in\ Cluster) * (Requests) = Load\ on\ Database$$

Additionally, updates to the database by one node will not be propagated to the cache state of other nodes in the cluster, resulting in stale reads. Obviously, the load on the database increases in proportion to the number of application server nodes in the cluster, but caching must also be taken into consideration; the more effective your caching strategy, the lesser the load on the database. That said, the database load is still multiplied by the number of nodes, even with an aggressive caching strategy. In effect, your caching efficacy is commensurately weakened as the number of nodes in your cluster increases.

When building applications that have objects that receive high volumes of writes, the solution is to remove the redundancy of maintaining a single cache per node, and instead move to a clustered caching configuration. There are several caching implementations that provide clustering capability, including Ehcache and Infinispan. For our discussion, we'll continue using Ehcache as our cache provider.

Cluster Caching and Replication Mechanics

Ehcache provides three different mechanisms for synchronizing each node's cache data. As data is persisted to one node's cache, the changes are broadcast to the other nodes in the cluster using a particular replication strategy. Ehcache supports replication via JMS, RMI, or JGroups. For all of these strategies, Ehcache does not attempt to use locking as a means to prevent data inconsistencies between nodes in the cluster.

This is likely done for performance considerations, and therefore your application should be able to deal with the potential for stale data.

When used in the basic clustered configuration, Ehcache does not distribute the entirety of cached data across each of the nodes in the cluster. Rather, each node contains a complete set of the cached data. While this does increase memory overhead, it improves performance by reducing network overhead. To reduce your application's memory footprint, you should adjust the maximum number of objects stored within each cache region. You should also consider the average size of each entity that might be stored within a particular cache region, because this impacts the memory utilization. We have seen memory issues creep up in cache configurations with a low number of cached items, due to the large size of each item stored in the cache. These factors are rarely given ample consideration, but are often the cause of significant bottlenecks.

Regardless of the replication mechanism, Ehcache provides two different strategies for actually notifying different nodes in the cluster of changes:

- The default strategy is to send the key of the cached item that was updated, along with the updated value. This strategy is called replicateUpdatesViaCopy, as the updated value is sent to all the other nodes in the cluster. While this approach is usually the fastest way to keep the different nodes in sync, it also carries the overhead of sending the updated value over the network. In cases where the updated value is quite large, this can have performance implications.

- An alternative is to just send a notification to the other nodes that they should invalidate the data in their respective caches. Then once the particular cache key has been invalidated, it will eventually be reloaded from the database on the next attempt to access that particular entity (or collection) for each of the nodes in the cluster. Obviously, this will incur additional load on the database—when a cache miss occurs on each of the other nodes in the cluster, they will need to requery the database to populate their respective caches. The advantage of this approach is that only the cache key needs to be transmitted to the other nodes.

The default replication behavior is to notify other nodes of changes asynchronously, allowing cache propagation to happen in the background and not affect the response time of the original operation (the notifier). In high-concurrency scenarios in which data coherency is a top priority, Ehcache can perform replication synchronously instead, preventing the cache operation from returning until the other nodes in the cluster have been successfully notified. Since this will have significant performance implications, it should be used only in specialized situations.

Configuring Replication

Ehcache clustering implementation does not require any changes to an application's code or architecture. You just need to modify the Ehcache configuration.

To get rolling with a clustered caching configuration for our example, we need to update our ehcache.xml file. We will select the JGroups replication mechanism. The following snippet is suggested by Ehcache's documentation:

```
<cacheManagerPeerProviderFactory
    class="net.sf.ehcache.distribution.jgroups
                            .JGroupsCacheManagerPeerProviderFactory"
        properties="connect=UDP(mcast_addr=231.12.21.132;mcast_port=45566;ip_ttl=32;
        mcast_send_buf_size=150000;mcast_recv_buf_size=80000):
        PING(timeout=2000;num_initial_members=6):
        MERGE2(min_interval=5000;max_interval=10000):
        FD_SOCK:VERIFY_SUSPECT(timeout=1500):
```

```
        pbcast.NAKACK(gc_lag=10;retransmit_timeout=3000):
        UNICAST(timeout=5000):
        pbcast.STABLE(desired_avg_gossip=20000):
        FRAG:
        pbcast.GMS(join_timeout=5000;join_retry_timeout=2000;
        shun=false;print_local_addr=true)"
        propertySeparator="::"
/>
```

These details specify the network and communication details for the JGroup implementation of Ehcache's cacheManagerPeerProviderFactory.

Next, we must add a cacheEventListenerFactory element to each of our cache regions. If we do not specify specific configuration for each cache region, we can just add this element to the default region configuration. Let's configure our Comment cache region as follows:

```
<cache name="com.apress.springpersistence.audiomanager.core.domain.Comment"
        maxElementsInMemory="5000"
        eternal="false"
        timeToIdleSeconds="900"
        timeToLiveSeconds="1800"
        overflowToDisk="false">

    <cacheEventListenerFactory
        class="net.sf.ehcache.distribution.jgroups
                                .JGroupsCacheReplicatorFactory"
        properties="replicateAsynchronously=true,
            replicatePuts=true,
            replicateUpdates=true,
            replicateUpdatesViaCopy=true,
            replicateRemovals=true"/>
</cache>
```

In this configuration, we set replicateAsynchronously to true, ensuring that updates happen asynchronously. Additionally, we set replicateUpdatesViaCopy to true, ensuring that the values of updated cache elements are sent directly to all of the other cluster nodes. Most of the other attributes should be fairly self-explanatory.

USING AN EXTERNAL CACHING SERVER

Another caching solution that limits the potential for coherency issues is to use a stand-alone cache server. Memcached, a popular open source memory object caching system, uses a similar strategy.

Ehcache provides a Cache Server implementation, which is a self-contained caching server that runs inside its own JVM. Because Cache Server is not tied to any particular node within your application cluster, there isn't much of a risk of version conflicts between caches (as there is only a single, external cache). If you are concerned about the caching server being a single point of failure, you can deploy it in a clustered configuration.

Using an external caching server can reduce the potential for inconsistencies in your cached data. However, you must weigh this against the penalty of network overhead, incurred from the fact that all calls to the caching server must be made over the network (rather than in process). Again, we recommend that you experiment with the various caching options, and pick the solution that is most ideal for your application's requirements.

Summary

In this chapter, we examined several strategies for evaluating and improving application performance. One of the most common pitfalls for Hibernate developers is the N+1 selects issue. This problem typically stems from a failure to properly tune a domain object's mapping configuration or the queries within the DAO layer. Understanding how this problem can appear, as well as how to detect it, is important in ensuring decent ORM performance. Although tuning really depends on the unique requirements of an application, often the best solution is to consider what data needs to be made available within the service, controller, or view layers, and optimize your queries to load this data as efficiently as possible. You saw that using a fetch-join is often an effective approach for initializing an association without requiring multiple queries. Relying on Hibernate's batching capability can also be a decent strategy, although it isn't always as effective.

Another technique for improving performance is to leverage Hibernate's caching capabilities. Properly tuning the cache can make a dramatic difference for application performance. However, caching can also degrade performance if it is not done correctly. For example, caching too aggressively can trigger OutOfMemoryException exceptions. Understanding the different caching configuration options within Hibernate will help you select the appropriate behavior. It is also important to experiment with different TTL settings.

Hibernate provides several different caching layers. The first-level cache is scoped at the EntityManager, but rarely requires much tuning. The second-level cache provides the ability to cache domain objects, collections, and queries. Each of these cache types is managed and cached separately. Domain objects are keyed by their identifier, and the values of all an object's properties are persisted to the cache. Associations and queries, however, persist only collections of identifiers. These identifiers are cross-referenced against the entity cache to load the actual domain object data.

Some cache implementations, such as Ehcache, are clusterable, allowing updates to the cache to be persisted to other nodes in the cluster. However, without a way to keep the caches of other nodes within the cluster in sync, there is the potential for significant problems, caused by version conflicts or stale data. For instance, it is possible for an important update applied to the database to be inadvertently rolled back. This can happen when a node's cache is not notified of the initial update to the database. Then, when a different user attempts to perform a write operation on the same entity, the user is applying his updates against stale data, which effectively rolls back the initial update once the second (stale) process is applied.

When deploying a clustered application, it is important to use a clusterable cache or a centralized cache server that all the nodes in the cluster can share. Ehcache provides a stand-alone server product called Cache Server. Additionally, Ehcache offers several configurable options for tuning its clusterable features. It is important to experiment with various settings to determine the options most suitable for your application's requirements.

Index

© Paul Fisher and Brian D. Murphy 2016
P. Fisher and B.D. Murphy, *Spring Persistence with Hibernate*, DOI 10.1007/978-1-4842-0268-5

Get the eBook for only $5!

Why limit yourself?

Now you can take the weightless companion with you wherever you go and access your content on your PC, phone, tablet, or reader.

Since you've purchased this print book, we're happy to offer you the eBook in all 3 formats for just $5.

Convenient and fully searchable, the PDF version enables you to easily find and copy code—or perform examples by quickly toggling between instructions and applications. The MOBI format is ideal for your Kindle, while the ePUB can be utilized on a variety of mobile devices.

To learn more, go to www.apress.com/companion or contact support@apress.com.

Printed in the United States
By Bookmasters